D1535914

LONGMAN

CORNERSTONE

B

Anna Uhl Chamot

Jim Cummins

Sharroky Hollie

PEARSON
Longman

Longman Cornerstone B

Pearson Education, 10 Bank Street, White Plains, NY 10606

Staff credits: The people who made up the *Longman Cornerstone* team, representing editorial, production, design, manufacturing, and marketing, are John Ade, Rhea Banker, Liz Barker, Kenna Bourke, Jeffrey Buckner, Brandon Carda, Daniel Comstock, Martina Deignan, Gina DiLillo, Nancy Flaggman, Cate Foley, Patrice Fraccio, Tracy Grenier, Zach Halper, Henry Hild, Sarah Hughes, Karen Kawaguchi, Lucille Kennedy, Ed Lamprich, Jamie Lawrence, Niki Lee, Christopher Leonowicz, Tara Maceyak, Katrinka Moore, Linda Moser, Liza Pleva, Edie Pullman, Monica Rodriguez, Tara Rose, Tania Saiz-Sousa, Chris Siley, Heather St. Clair, Loretta Steeves, and Andrew Vaccaro.

Text design and composition: The Quarasan Group, Inc.
Illustration and photo credits: See page 361.

Library of Congress Cataloging-in-Publication Data
Chamot, Anna Uhl.
  Longman Cornerstone / Anna Uhl Chamot, Jim Cummins, Sharroky Hollie.
  p. cm.
  Includes index.
  Contents: 1. Level 1. —2. Level 2. — A. Level 3. — B. Level 4. — C. Level 5.
  1. English language—Textbooks for foreign speakers. (1. English language—Textbooks for foreign speakers. 2. Readers.) I. Cummins, Jim. II. Hollie, Sharroky. III. Title.

ISBN-13: 978-0-13-514806-8
ISBN-10: 0-13-514806-5

Printed in the United States of America

2 3 4 5 6 7 8 9 10–CRK–12 11 10 09 08

Anna Uhl Chamot is a professor of secondary education and a faculty advisor for ESL in George Washington University's Department of Teacher Preparation. She has been a researcher and teacher trainer in content-based, second-language learning and language-learning strategies. She co-designed and has written extensively about the Cognitive Academic Language Learning Approach (CALLA) and spent seven years implementing the CALLA model in the Arlington Public Schools in Virginia.

Jim Cummins is the Canada Research Chair in the Department of Curriculum, Teaching, and Learning of the Ontario Institute for Studies in Education at the University of Toronto. His research focuses on literacy development in multilingual school contexts, as well as on the potential roles of technology in promoting language and literacy development. His recent publications include: *The International Handbook of English Language Teaching* (co-edited with Chris Davison) and *Literacy, Technology, and Diversity: Teaching for Success in Changing Times* (with Kristin Brown and Dennis Sayers).

Sharroky Hollie is an assistant professor in teacher education at California State University, Dominguez Hills. His expertise is in the field of professional development, African-American education, and second-language methodology. He is an urban literacy visiting professor at Webster University, St. Louis. Sharroky is the Executive Director of the Center for Culturally Responsive Teaching and Learning (CCRTL) and the co-founding director of the nationally-acclaimed Culture and Language Academy of Success (CLAS).

Consultants and Reviewers

Rebecca Anselmo
Sunrise Acres Elementary School
Las Vegas, NV

Ana Applegate
Redlands School District
Redlands, CA

Terri Armstrong
Houston ISD
Houston, TX

Jacqueline Avritt
Riverside County Office of Ed.
Hemet, CA

Mitchell Bobrick
Palm Beach County School
West Palm Beach, FL

Victoria Brioso-Saldala
Broward County Schools
Fort Lauderdale, FL

Brenda Cabarga Schubert
Creekside Elementary School
Salinas, CA

Joshua Ezekiel
Bardin Elementary School
Salinas, CA

Veneshia Gonzalez
Seminole Elementary School
Okeechobee, FL

Carolyn Grigsby
San Francisco Unified School District
San Francisco, CA

Julie Grubbe
Plainfield Consolidated Schools
Chicago, IL

Yasmin Hernandez-Manno
Newark Public Schools
Newark, NJ

Janina Kusielewicz
Clifton Public Schools/Bilingual Ed.
& Basic Skills Instruction Dept.
Clifton, NJ

Mary Helen Lechuga
El Paso ISD
El Paso, TX

Gayle P. Malloy
Randolph School District
Randolph, MA

Randy Payne
Patterson/Taft Elementaries
Mesa, AZ

Marcie L. Schnegelberger
Alisal Union SD
Salinas, CA

Lorraine Smith
Collier County Schools
Naples, FL

Shawna Stoltenborg
Glendale Elementary School
Glen Burnie, MD

Denise Tiffany
West High School
Iowa City, IO

Dear Student,

Welcome to Longman Cornerstone!

We wrote *Longman Cornerstone* to help you succeed in all your school studies. This program will help you learn the English language you need to study language arts, social studies, math, and science. You will learn how to speak to family members, classmates, and teachers in English.

Cornerstone includes a mix of many subjects. Each unit has four different readings that include some fiction (made-up) and nonfiction (true) articles, stories, songs, and poems. The readings will give you some of the tools you need to do well in all your subjects in school.

As you use this program, you will build on what you already know and learn new words, new information and facts, and take part in creative activities. The activities will help you improve your English skills.

Learning a language takes time, but just like learning to skateboard or learning to swim, it is fun!

We hope you enjoy *Longman Cornerstone* as much as we enjoyed writing it for you!

Good luck!

Anna Uhl Chamot
Jim Cummins
Sharroky Hollie

A *Cornerstone* Unit Walkthrough

Your *Cornerstone* Unit!

Cornerstones are important for a building and important for learning, too.

Meet the program that will give you the cornerstones you need to improve in English and do better in all your subjects in school.

Kick Off Each Unit

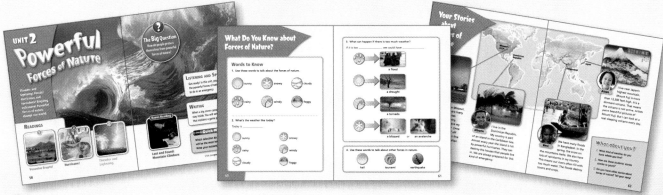

Big Question
The Big Question pulls all the readings together and helps you focus on big ideas.

Words to Know
Learn new vocabulary for the unit theme.

Mini-Autobiographies
Meet other students, and hear what they say about the unit theme.

For Each Reading

Vocabulary
Get to know the words *before* you read.

Readings ①, ②, and ③
Read with success! Get help from glossed words and check-up questions.

After Each Reading

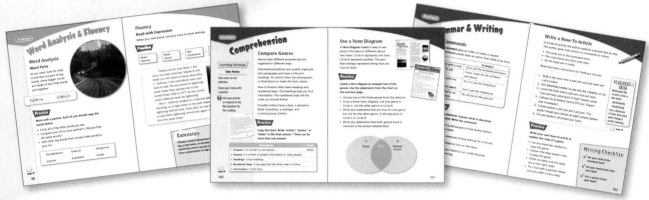

Word Analysis & Fluency
Become a better reader by learning about phonics and how words are formed. Then practice reading with ease on fluency pages.

Comprehension
Focus on a comprehension skill and practice it using a graphic organizer.

Grammar & Writing
Learn rules of grammar to help you communicate. Then improve your writing skills.

Wrap Up Each Unit

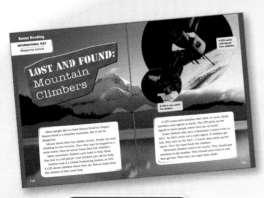

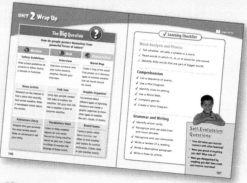

Bonus Reading
Take a break and read for fun.

? Wrap up
Discuss the Big Question with your class. Choose an Assessment Project to show all you have learned.

UNIT 1

Contents

Animals, People, and Caring

? The Big Question

Powerful Forces of Nature

? The **Big** Question

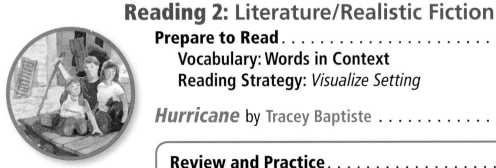

UNIT 3

Contents

Telling Tales

? The Big Question

UNIT 4

Contents

Problem Solvers

? The Big Question

City Council
Josefina
Aranda

Contents

Where We Live

Contents

UNIT 6 — Links to Our Past

Reading 3: Literature/Realistic Fiction

Bonus Reading: Informational Text/Social Studies

Unit Wrap Up

Handbook

UNIT 1

Animals, People, and Caring

Animals are fun to be around. Some keep us company. Other animals help us. It is important to take care of our animal friends.

READINGS

1

Taking Care of the Young

2

The Presidents' Pets

3

The Star Llama

LISTENING AND SPEAKING

In this unit, you will tell your own pet story.

Bonus Reading

Wild Horses

WRITING

You will describe how to care for something or someone.

Quick Write

Why do you think people like having pets? Write your reasons.

What Do You Know about Animals?

Words to Know

1. Use these words to talk about animals.

 alligator

 raccoon

 elephant

 parrot

 skunk

 giraffe

2. What are some wild animals?

_____ *is a wild animal.*

 An alligator

 A skunk

 A parrot

 An elephant

 A raccoon

 A giraffe

3. Where do animals live?

The _____ *lives in* _____ .

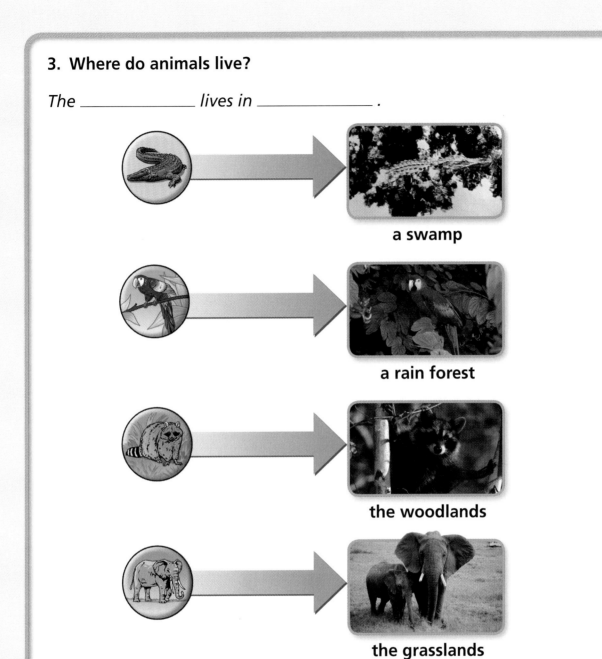

a swamp

a rain forest

the woodlands

the grasslands

4. Use these words to talk about other animals.

lion

snake

zebra

hippopotamus

Your Stories about Animals

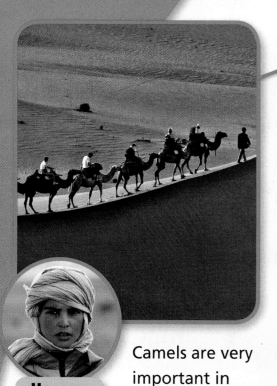

Hassan

Camels are very important in Morocco. They help us cross the desert. Camels can live for days without water. When they get thirsty, we give them water.

Cassandra

I live on Santorini. It is an island in Greece. The streets are very steep. Our donkeys carry people and packages. I brush my donkey to keep him clean.

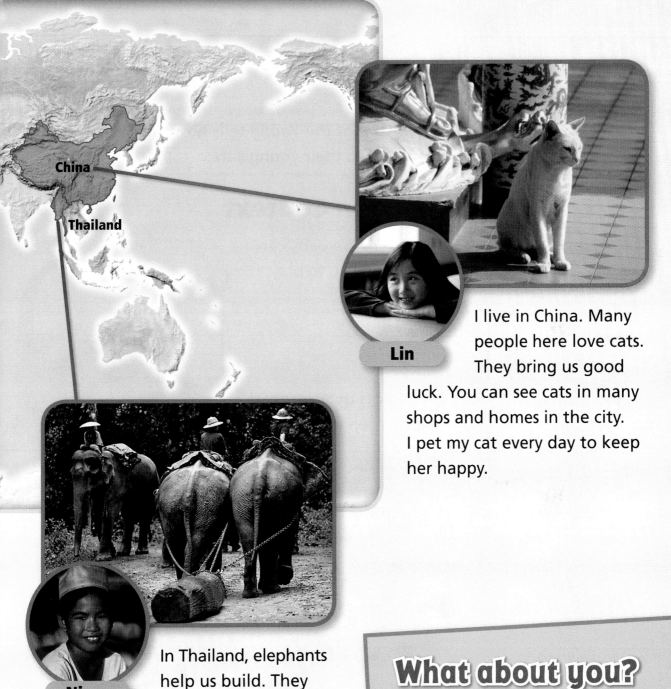

China

Thailand

Lin

I live in China. Many people here love cats. They bring us good luck. You can see cats in many shops and homes in the city. I pet my cat every day to keep her happy.

Niran

In Thailand, elephants help us build. They carry heavy loads on their backs. They can lift things with their strong trunks. They can also drag heavy loads. I feed my elephants grass and leaves. This food keeps them strong and healthy.

What about you?

1 Which animal do you like the most? Why?

2 How are these stories similar to yours?

3 Do you have a story about animals? Tell your story!

Vocabulary

Taking Care of the Young tells how different animals keep their young safe.

Words in Context

1 Kittens are baby cats. The **young** like to play.

2 Parents try to **protect** their children from danger.

Key Words

young

protect

secure

communicates

3 Animals keep their young **secure**.

4 A dog **communicates** by barking and by using its tail and ears.

Practice

Use each key word in a sentence.

Make Connections

Sometimes, animals need our help. Have you ever helped an animal? How?

Academic Words

involve

include, be a part of

require

need

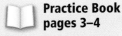
Practice Book pages 3–4

INFORMATIONAL TEXT

Science

The Big Question

Why is it important to take care of the young?

Reading Strategy

Reread

Before you read:

- Ask yourself: What do I already know? What do I want to find out?
- Copy the chart on page 23. Fill in the first two columns.

After you read:

- Reread parts of the story. This helps you remember what you learned.
- Later, you will fill in the last column of the chart.

Taking Care of the Young

Adult penguins watch their chicks.

Penguins

Human babies need adults to protect them. Animal babies need parents, too.

Both male and female emperor penguins take care of their babies. The mother lays an egg. Then the father keeps the egg warm while the mother looks for food.

Emperor penguin chicks stay close to their parents at all times after they are born. One parent will stay and watch the chicks. The other will go find food. Then he or she will bring the food back for the babies to eat. The parents work together to keep their babies safe.

---

human   person

female   girl or woman

Check Up   Who gets the food for baby penguins? If you don't know, reread this page.

11

Swans

Swans also take care of their young. One parent stays with the cygnets at all times. This keeps the babies safe. The cygnets cannot fly for many months after they are born. It is hard for cygnets to escape danger on their own when they cannot fly.

The adult swans work hard to keep animals away from their cygnets. They also teach their babies how to take care of themselves. Soon, the cygnets will be old enough to fly. Then they will leave their parents.

---

cygnets   baby swans

danger   anything that can cause harm or pain

This mother swan watches her cygnets.

Raccoons

Raccoon babies are very small when they are born. They cannot stand or open their eyes. Only female raccoons take care of the babies. A mother might have four babies to take care of alone. She must leave them in the den when she looks for food. In the den, the raccoon babies are safe from danger.

The mother raccoon worries that other animals might find her den. So after a few months, the family moves. By then, the babies can walk and climb. Their mother has taught them to take care of themselves.

---

den   home for animals that is hidden

Baby raccoons wait for their mother in their den.

CheckUp Reread the last paragraph. Why does the mother move the family?

Wallabies

Mother wallabies have an unusual way to protect their babies. They carry their babies in a pouch. A baby wallaby, called a joey, has no fur when it is born. The baby climbs into its mother's pouch to stay warm. The wallaby's pouch also guards the joey from danger.

When a joey gets older, it will sometimes leave its mother's pouch. But mother wallabies still watch their babies to keep them safe. If a mother wallaby senses trouble, she communicates with her baby. She stomps on the ground. This tells her joey to return to her pouch.

---

pouch   pocket used to carry things

guards   protects or keeps safe

This baby wallaby is protected in its mother's pouch.

Clown Fish

All animal parents have to be careful. Even fish parents watch for danger in the water. Clown fish fathers guard their eggs carefully to keep them safe. They keep other fish away from their eggs. They also keep the eggs clean.

After the eggs hatch, the babies want to swim and find food. The fish babies swim away from their parents. Now they are on their own. Soon, they will find a place to live. Later, they will become parents themselves. They will have their own eggs to protect.

---

hatch   come out of an egg

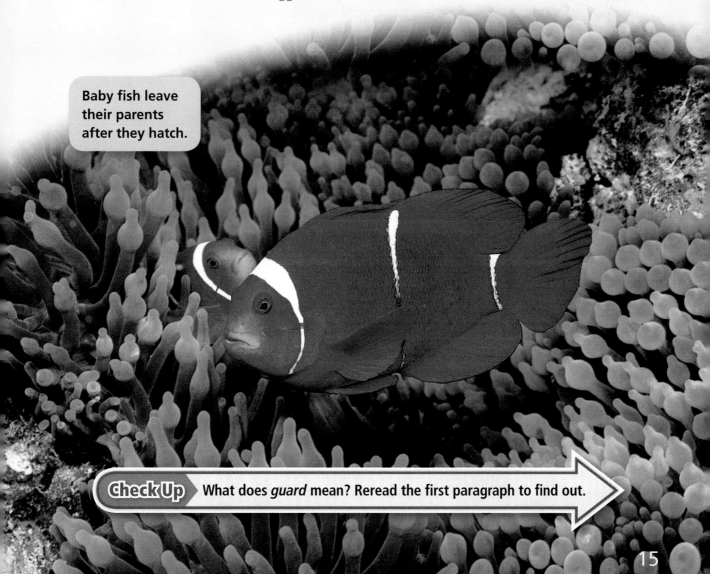

Baby fish leave their parents after they hatch.

Check Up   What does *guard* mean? Reread the first paragraph to find out.

15

People

Human mothers and fathers take care of their young. They must watch their children carefully. When it is cold, they put hats and sweaters on their children to keep them warm. Sometimes, they carry their kids in their arms or on their shoulders.

Human children and animal babies keep their parents busy! How are these animals just like people?

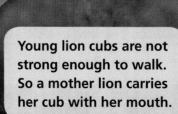

Young lion cubs are not strong enough to walk. So a mother lion carries her cub with her mouth.

A penguin keeps its chick warm in the cold.

A bear cub likes to play and run. Its mother needs to watch it carefully.

Practice Book pages 5–6

Reading Strategy

Reread

Sometimes it helps to go back and reread parts of a story.

- Did it help you to reread parts of this selection? How?

- What did you learn when you reread?

Think It Over

1 Name the animals in this selection.

2 What does a cygnet become when it grows up?

3 Who takes care of the clown fish eggs? How?

4 How do wallabies keep their babies safe?

Animals
and Their Young

▲ **Goose and goslings**
This mother goose has
two goslings.

▲ **Lion and cub**
A mother lion keeps her cub clean.

◀ **Horse and foal**
A horse runs with her
new foal.

▲ Eagle and chick

An eagle feeds its chick. They live in a nest high in a tree.

▲ Hyena and pups

A hyena is in the dog family. Its babies are also called pups.

▲ Deer and fawn

A young deer is called a fawn. It has spots to help it hide in the woods.

▲ Cow and calf

The young calf stands in a field with two cows.

Activity to Do!

These two pages told you about adult animals and their babies.

- Choose an animal.
- Research the animal.
- Tell about that animal's babies using pictures and words.

Phonics & Fluency

Phonics

Short Vowels

Each word in the chart has one vowel. Read the words.

a	e	i	o	u
can	get	big	fox	cub
bag	den	his	not	pup

Rule Box

A word is likely to have a short vowel sound when:

- it has a single vowel.
- the vowel has a single consonant before and after it.

c a n	g e t	p u p
C V C	C V C	C V C

Practice

Work with a partner. Copy the chart.

- Find the CVC word or words in each sentence.
- List each CVC word in the correct column.

1. I fed my cat today.
2. Horses like to rub noses.
3. A chicken can be a family pet.
4. A group of whales is a pod.
5. A pig can run in a pen.

Short Vowel Sound				
a	e	i	o	u

Fluency

Read with Expression

When you read aloud, use your voice to show feelings.

Practice

| Read silently. | ▷ | Read aloud. | ▷ | Get comments. | ▷ | Read aloud again. |

Raccoon babies are very small when they are born. They cannot stand or open their eyes. Only female raccoons take care of the babies. A mother might have four babies to take care of alone. She must leave them in the den when she looks for food. In the den, the raccoon babies are safe from danger.

The mother raccoon worries that other animals might find her den. So after a few months, the family moves. By then, the babies can walk and climb. Their mother has taught them to take care of themselves.

Extension

Choose one animal. Find pictures of the baby animal with its mother. Create a poster. Share your poster with your class.

Comprehension

Reread for Details

You can reread a selection to find information.

Summarize

Summarize the selection for a partner.

 Ask your partner to respond to the Big Question for this reading.

Practice

Tell if each statement below is TRUE or FALSE. Tell the page number you found the answer on.

1. Only the male emperor penguin takes care of penguin chicks.
2. Cygnets leave their parents when they can fly.
3. Only female raccoons take care of baby raccoons.
4. The father clown fish shows the babies how to swim.

Practice Book page 8

22

Use a KWL Chart

A KWL Chart helps you remember three kinds of information:

1. What you **Know** about a topic before reading

2. What you **Want** to learn about the topic

3. What you **Learned** about the topic

Practice

Before reading, you completed the first two columns.
Now complete the third column: What I Learned.

- Begin by adding new details you remember.
- Then look back in the selection to recall other details.

Topic: Taking care of the young		
What I Know	**What I Want to Learn**	**What I Learned**
		The mother wallaby's pouch protects her baby.

1. What is something that you still want to learn about how animals care for their young?

2. Where might you look to find this information?

Extension

Form a small group and pick a favorite animal. Write a skit about that animal and its babies.

Grammar & Writing

Plural Nouns

Some words that name young animals are: *chicks*, *cubs*, and *babies*. All of these words are plural nouns. **Plural nouns** name two or more people, places, things, or animals.

Rules	Examples		
To form the plural of most nouns, add -*s*.	chick	→	chicks
	raccoon	→	raccoons
	eye	→	eyes
To form the plural of nouns ending in *s*, *ss*, *ch*, *sh*, or *x*, add -*es*.	pouch	→	pouches
	bush	→	bushes
	fox	→	foxes
To form the plural of nouns ending in a consonant and *y*, change the *y* to *i* and add -*es*.	baby	→	babies
	family	→	families
	body	→	bodies

Practice

Copy each singular noun. Write the plural form of the noun.

1. puppy

2. egg

3. inch

4. brush

5. enemy

6. place

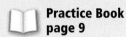
Practice Book page 9

Write a How-To Description

Read what Jason wrote about how to take care of a pet. As you read, pay special attention to the order words. Notice how the actions are explained in order.

I have a dog called Sparks. Every morning, I take him for a short walk. We walk around the neighborhood. Next, I feed him. Then, I go to school. When I come back from school, I take Sparks for a long walk. When he is tired, we go home. Later, I feed him again. At night, Sparks goes to his bed and falls asleep.

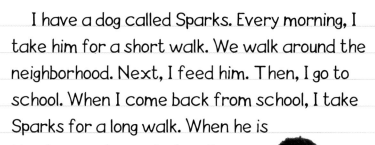

SPELLING TIP

Notice that the word *him* has the CVC pattern. Can you find other CVC words in the paragraph? Remember to use the CVC pattern when you write.

📖 **Practice Book page 10**

Practice

Write a how-to description. Think of something or someone you take care of.

- Name the person or thing you take care of.
- Make a list of the steps you take.
- Write a paragraph. Make sure you put the steps in order.

Writing Checklist

✓ Is your topic clear?

✓ Do the steps make sense?

✓ Can a partner understand how you take care of the person or thing you wrote about?

The Presidents' PETS

Vocabulary

The Presidents' Pets is about some of the animals that have lived in the White House.

Words in Context

1 A giraffe is an **unusual** pet.

2 These girls are **dedicated** to their pet. They spend time taking care of it.

3 The president lives in the Executive Mansion — also known as the White House. **Executive** means head, or chief.

Key Words

unusual
dedicated
executive
capital
museum
memorabilia

26

4 This map shows California. The red star shows where the state **capital** is.

5 Children learn about art at this **museum**.

6 Travelers like to buy **memorabilia**. It helps them remember the places they visit.

Practice

Use each key word in a sentence.

Make Connections

Tell about pets you know.

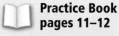

Practice Book pages 11–12

INFORMATIONAL TEXT

Magazine Article

The Big Question

Why do you think our presidents have pets to take care of?

Reading Strategy

Preview

- Read the title.
- Study the photographs and the captions.
- Predict what this selection will be about.

The Presidents' PETS

George W. Bush had a black terrier named Barney.

When is the White House more like a zoo? When the president, his or her family, and all of their pets move in!

Even the White House guards loved President Coolidge's cat, Tiger.

First Lady Grace Coolidge holds Rebecca, her pet raccoon.

Animals that run, jump, hop, swim, and fly have lived in the Executive Mansion. That is another name for the White House. The president's home in Washington, D.C., is not a zoo. But many exotic pets have lived there.

Calvin Coolidge and his wife had a cat named Tiger. But they also were dedicated to a raccoon named Rebecca. The president often walked this strange pet outside at night.

John Quincy Adams owned an alligator. Theodore Roosevelt had a zebra, a lion, a hyena, and many other pets!

---

exotic very different or unusual

CheckUp Where is the White House?

29

William Howard Taft's cow gave him milk every day.

John F. Kennedy's family had dogs and cats. They also had ducks, rabbits, and even a pony.

Many people wrote letters to famous White House pets. But only Warren Harding's dog, Laddie Boy, "wrote" newspaper stories. A writer described life in our nation's capital from the dog's point of view.

Some White House pets have helped our country. During a time of war, Woodrow Wilson's family kept sheep. By eating grass, the sheep mowed the White House lawn. William Howard Taft's cow, Pauline, supplied the president's milk every morning.

---

described   told about

The Kennedy children had a pony. It was just one of their many pets.

George Washington, our country's first president, owned a parrot.

Do you want to learn more about animals that have lived with our presidents' families? You can visit the Presidential Pet Museum. It is located in Annapolis, Maryland.

The museum displays memorabilia of many White House pets. There is a statue of Fala, Franklin Delano Roosevelt's terrier. You also can find a cowbell there. The bell hung from the neck of the last cow to live at the White House.

Presidential pets from coyotes to owls have lived in the White House. Frogs and lizards have lived there, too. The White House has been home to some unusual pets!

---

presidential   like or relating to a president

displays   shows

Practice Book
pages 13–14

Reading Strategy

Preview

Before reading, you previewed the selection.

- What did the title and photographs tell you about the selection?
- Did previewing help you when you read? How?

Think It Over

1 Which president had an alligator?

2 Where is the Presidential Pet Museum?

3 Which White House pet is the most unusual? Why?

31

Phonics & Fluency

Phonics

Long Vowels with Silent *e*

The words in the chart follow the CVCe pattern.

a_e	i_e	o_e	u_e
cane	like	note	cube
made	time	home	cute
gate	life	hope	mule

Rule Box

When the first vowel in a one-syllable word is followed by both a consonant and an e, the vowel is usually long. The final e is silent.

c a n e   l i k e   c u b e
C V C e   C V C e   C V C e

Practice

Work with a partner.

1. Read the CVC words aloud.

2. Add an e to each word to write a CVCe word.

3. Read the CVCe words aloud.

CVC Words	CVCe Words
bit	
cod	
fad	
fin	

Practice Book

page 15

Fluency
Read for Speed and Accuracy

You should read quickly. But never read so quickly that you lose your understanding.

Practice

| Read for one minute. | Count the words you read. | Study any hard words. | Read and count again. |

Animals that run, jump, hop, swim, and fly have lived in the	12
Executive Mansion. That is another name for the White House.	22
The president's home in Washington, D.C., is not a zoo. But	33
many exotic pets have lived there.	39
Calvin Coolidge and his wife had a cat named Tiger. But they	51
also were dedicated to a raccoon named Rebecca. The president	61
often walked this strange pet outside at night.	69
John Quincy Adams owned an alligator. Theodore Roosevelt	77
had a zebra, a lion, a hyena, and many other pets!	88
John F. Kennedy's family had dogs and cats. They also had	99
ducks, rabbits, and even a pony.	105
Many people wrote letters to famous White House pets.	114
But only Warren Harding's dog, Laddie Boy, "wrote" newspaper	123
stories. A writer described life in our nation's capital from the	134
dog's point of view.	138

Extension

Write an email or a letter to any elected official to find out about their pets. Ask them to send you pictures of their pets. Share the information with your class.

Comprehension

Preview

Before you read the selection, you previewed
it. When readers preview a story, they look at:

- **titles**
- **subtitles**
- **photos or illustrations**
- **captions**

Previewing helps readers understand a
story. It tells you a little about the topic.
Then you have some information about
the topic before you start reading.

Practice

1. When you previewed this selection, what
   did the pictures and captions tell you?

2. Turn to page 40. Preview the text. What
   do you think it will be about?

3. Now turn to page 52. Preview the text.
   What will this text be about?

📖 **Practice Book**
page 16

Use a Details Chart

You can use a Details Chart to collect specific information from a text.

Copy this Details Chart. Write the names of the presidents mentioned in the selection. Then add details about their pets.

President		Detail 1	Detail 2
Calvin Coolidge	→	cat (Tiger)	raccoon (Rebecca)
	→		
	→		
	→		
	→		
	→		
	→		
	→		

1. How does the Details Chart help you find information?

2. Check your chart. Who was Pauline?

Grammar & Writing

Common Nouns and Proper Nouns

Common nouns are used to name any person, place, thing, or animal: *dog*, *house*, *boy*.

Proper nouns name specific people, places, things, or animals: *Laddie Boy*, *White House*, *John*.

Proper nouns always begin with a capital letter. Sometimes a proper noun has more than one word.

Common Nouns	Proper Nouns
pet	Laddie Boy, Tiger
president	John F. Kennedy
museum	Presidential Pet Museum
city	Annapolis
state	Maryland

Practice

Write two proper nouns for each common noun.

1. store

2. president

3. school

4. country

5. book

6. state

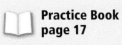
Practice Book page 17

Write a Description

A **description** is a picture made of words. When you describe something, you give details that tell how it looks. You also can tell about how it sounds or acts. Good writers use sense words to tell how something sounds, smells, tastes, feels, looks, and acts.

Read Ernesto's description of an iguana.

I was on the subway going home. I saw something very strange. A man sat in front of me and took something out of his bag. It was an animal. It was on a leash, but it was not a dog. It looked like a big lizard. It had huge eyes and a long tail. Its body was green, and its skin looked bumpy. It did not make any noise. It was an iguana!

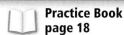

SPELLING TIP

Can you find any CVCe words in the paragraph? Remember to use the CVCe pattern when you write.

Practice Book page 18

Practice

Think about your pet or the pet of someone you know. Write a paragraph describing that pet.

- What kind of animal is it?
- How does it look?
- How does it act?
- What sounds does it make?

Writing Checklist

✓ Did you describe a pet?

✓ Did you include enough details?

✓ Did you capitalize all proper nouns?

✓ Can a partner picture the animal you described?

The Star Llama

Vocabulary

The Star Llama is about a boy and his llama.

Words in Context

Key Words

- shimmer
- frisky
- glowed
- warm
- breath
- companion

1 See the sunlight **shimmer** on the surface of the water.

2 Many young animals are **frisky**. Just like human children, they love to play.

3 The fireflies **glowed** in the jar.

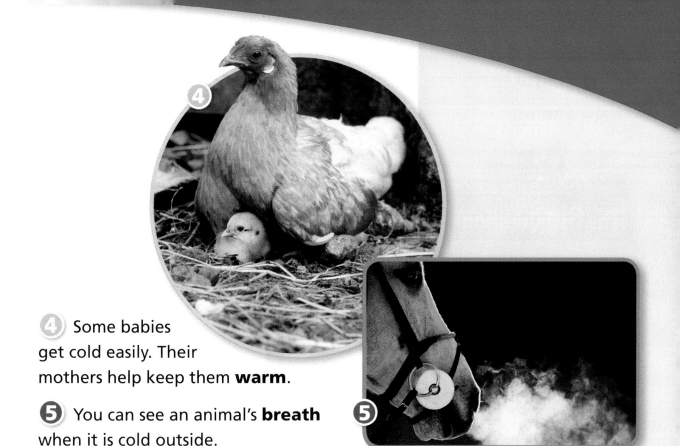

4 Some babies get cold easily. Their mothers help keep them **warm**.

5 You can see an animal's **breath** when it is cold outside.

6 A pet can be a good **companion**. This puppy keeps these people company on a picnic.

Practice

Use each key word in a sentence.

Make Connections

In the next story, the boy's special friend is a llama. Have you ever had a real or stuffed animal as a special friend?

Academic Words

partner
someone who works with you on an activity

bond
special relationship or connection

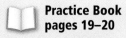
Practice Book pages 19–20

The Big Question

In what ways can animals help the people who care for them?

Reading Strategy

Identify Fantasy and Reality

Many stories tell of events that can happen in real life. But sometimes, stories tell of things that could never happen in reality.

- Read the title.
- Look at the pictures.
- Think of the story parts that could be real.
- Think of the story parts that must be fantasy.

The Star Llama

by Jan Mike
illustrated by Theresa Smith

Once there was a young Inca boy. He had no family except for an old llama. Each day, the boy and his companion walked many miles, looking for a home. Each night, they curled up together and slept. But one starry evening, the old llama died.

Inca   person who lives in the Andes mountains in South America

llama   South American animal with thick hair like wool and a long neck

Check Up > Could the events in this picture really happen? ➤

41

The boy buried his friend next to an icy stream. Then he sat under a tree and cried. What would he do, he thought. He had no family and no home.

The boy cried for a very long time. But there was no one to comfort him. There were only the stars in the sky.

---

stream   flow of water that moves across the land and is narrower than a river

Suddenly, the sky filled with bright light. The boy held his breath. He was afraid to move. One star began to shimmer. Then it floated to the ground beside the stream. Slowly, the star took the shape of the old llama. The llama bent her head and drank from the stream.

CheckUp Could the events in this picture really happen?

The star llama drank for a very long time. Then she looked at the sad Inca boy and smiled. When she jumped back into the sky, bits of llama wool fell. The boy felt the silver wool. It was soft and warm.

As the sun began to rise, the boy gathered the llama wool. It glowed in his hands like starlight. He carried the wool to the city and sold it. With the money, he bought a house and two frisky young llamas. He never forgot the star llama. And he was never lonely again.

---

gathered   collected

Practice Book
pages 21–22

Reading Strategy

Identify Fantasy and Reality

- Which parts of the story could be real?
- Which parts are fantasy?
- Did telling fantasy from reality help you understand the story? How?

Think It Over

1 Where does this story take place?

2 Why does the boy cry?

3 How does the old llama come back?

4 How does the boy buy a house and two llamas?

45

Word Analysis & Fluency

Word Analysis

Endings: *-s, -es, -ed*

A **verb** names an action. The ending of a verb tells when the action happened.

> Today the boy **walks** many miles without his llama.
>
> Now the boy **searches** for the star llama.
>
> Yesterday, the boy **walked** many miles.

Rule Box

walks = walk + *s*   searches = search + *es*

walked = walk + *ed*

The endings *-s* and *-es* tell what the boy does now.
The ending *-ed* tells what the boy did in the past.

Practice

Work with a partner. Take turns reading the sentences below.

- Charlie the llama plays in a field.
- His hair reaches down to the ground.
- Charlie wanted to visit new places.
- He runs around the yard.

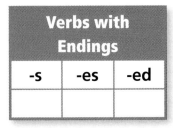

Verbs with Endings		
-s	-es	-ed

1. List each verb in the correct column.

2. Look back in the story. Find three words ending in *-ed*.

Fluency

Look Ahead

Sometimes readers look for hard words before they read. They then try to figure them out.

Practice

| Pick one passage. | → | Find any hard words. | → | Practice saying those words. | → | Read the passage aloud. |

1 A boy had a llama as his companion. The old llama died, and the boy was sad. Then the boy had good luck. He bought a home, and he was happy.

2 Suddenly, the sky filled with bright light. The boy held his breath. He was afraid to move. One star began to shimmer. Then it floated to the ground beside the stream.

3 As the sun began to rise, the boy gathered the llama wool. It glowed in his hands like starlight. He carried the wool to the city and sold it. With the money, he bought a house and two frisky young llamas. He never forgot the star llama. And he was never lonely again.

Comprehension

Learning Strategy

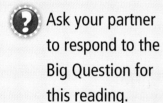

Retell

Retell the story to a partner.

? Ask your partner to respond to the Big Question for this reading.

Fantasy and Reality

Some stories are **fantasy**, or make-believe. The characters or the settings are not real. The events could never happen.

Other stories are **realistic**. They are based on reality, or the real world. The events could happen. Some stories have both fantasy and reality in them.

Practice

Read each sentence. Ask yourself, *Could this really happen?*

- If the answer is yes, write R for reality.
- If the answer is no, write F for fantasy.

1. A boy and a llama walk many miles in the Andes Mountains.
2. The boy goes to sleep next to his llama.
3. The boy sits under a tree and cries.
4. A star takes the shape of a llama.
5. The star llama drinks from the stream.

📖 **Practice Book page 24**

Use a Fantasy and Reality Chart

A Fantasy and Reality Chart helps readers understand a story that has both fantasy and reality. It also helps readers look more closely at the characters, setting, or plot of a story.

Practice

Copy the chart. Write the sentences from the previous page in the correct column. Then reread the story. Find another sentence for the Fantasy column and another sentence for the Reality column.

Fantasy	Reality
	A boy and a llama walk many miles in the Andes Mountains.

Compare your chart with a partner's. Discuss what makes *The Star Llama* a fantasy story and not realistic fiction.

Grammar & Writing

Subject and Object Pronouns

The words *he* and *him* are pronouns. **Pronouns** take the place of nouns. Pronouns are very useful. Without them, we would have to keep repeating words like *the boy* over and over.

> **Subject pronouns** are used as subjects in sentences.
> *I, you, he, she, it, we, they*
> **He** had no family except for an old llama.
>
> **Object pronouns** are used as objects in sentences.
> *me, you, him, her, it, us, them*
> There was no one to comfort **him**.

Practice

Read the sentences. Write each subject and object pronoun.

1. The boy loved the old llama. He was sad when she died.

2. He missed her very much.

3. One star began to shimmer. Then it floated to the ground.

4. The star llama smiled at the boy. Then she jumped back into the sky.

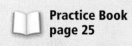

**Practice Book
page 25**

50

Write a Description of an Event

To describe an event, you have to explain what happened and who did what. The characters are important in the description. They experience the events of the story.

Read Michael's description of a fantasy event. Pay special attention to the characters.

Spot is my pet. He plays in our garden when I am in school. Everyone knows he is a special dog. One day, my mom was in the kitchen looking for something. She slipped and broke her arm. Spot barked for help. Nobody was home to help her. So, Spot drove Mom to the hospital. Now, he wants to drive the car every day.

SPELLING TIP

Many present-tense verbs have the ending *-s* or *-es*. Many past-tense verbs have the ending *-ed*. Remember to add *-s*, *-es*, and *-ed* when you write.

Practice Book page 26

Practice

Write a description of an event. Your event should be part reality and part fantasy.

- Choose your characters.
- Think of events that could happen in real life.
- Think of at least one event that is make-believe.

Writing Checklist

✓ Did you tell about the events in the order they could have happened?

✓ Did you use character traits for your main character?

✓ Did you include both real and fantasy parts?

✓ Can a partner tell what is real and what is fantasy?

Wild

You have seen horses in many different places. Maybe you have seen them on a farm. Or you have seen police riding horses in the city. These horses are not wild. They work and live around people every day.

Other horses are naturally wild. They have never lived around people. They live in nature and run in herds. Herd animals live in groups. Wild horses do not work for people. They roam the land in nature and care for themselves.

Horses

This herd of horses runs free in the wild.

Some wild horses are not really wild. The mustang is an example of this. Mustangs lived and worked with people in the past. But some mustangs ran away and now live in the wild. People call these horses wild, but they are not true wild horses.

One type of wild horse is called Przewalski's horse. This kind of horse has always been wild. Other breeds of wild horses became extinct. That means they no longer exist. Not long ago, the Przewalski's horse was almost extinct. In 1945 there were only 31 left of the breed. Today, about 1,500 of these horses live in the wild.

There are not many places where wild horses can live. Their land was used for houses and farms. Most wild horses now live in zoos. Not long ago, zoos were the only place to find wild horses. But people worked hard to save these animals. They returned them to the wild.

At first it was hard for these horses to live on their own. But people are helping the horses learn to live in nature. They want these horses to be wild again. Now there are more wild horses running free.

Wild horses live in herds and do not work for people.

54

Horses spend their days running, eating, and sleeping. In zoos and on farms, people take care of horses. In the wild, horses help each other. Mares, or female horses, groom their foals to keep them clean. Herds run together in the wild to stay safe.

Wild horses need to run far to look for food. Some western states let horses run and graze, or eat grass, on public land. The government wants to help and protect wild horses.

Most of us do not see wild horses running free. But they are there. Hopefully, over time, there will be more of them.

The Big Question

How do animals and people show they care?

Written	**Oral**	**Visual/Active**
Science Article	**Presentation**	**Picture Book**
Research an animal. Write information about how that animal cares for its young.	Prepare a lesson to share what you learned about an animal and its young. Present your lesson to classmates.	Create a picture book. Find photos that show how human parents and animal parents are similar.
Parenting Brochure	**Interview**	**Animal Playing Cards**
Create a brochure to help animal parents. Choose an animal. Describe the special needs of that animal's babies.	Interview someone who has a pet. Find out how that person cares for their animal. Record your interview.	Create matching cards: one set for adult animals; the other for their young. Write the animal names. Use your cards to play games.
Adventure Story	**Question Game**	**Poster**
Write a story about a young animal that gets into trouble. Tell how its parent saves it. Make sure your story is based on facts about the animal.	Create questions about special ways animals take care of babies. Record your questions on index cards. Use the cards to play a question game.	Create a poster to decorate the classroom. The poster will give examples of animals taking care of their young.

✔ Learning Checklist

Word Analysis and Phonics

✓ Read words with short vowels.

✓ Read words with long vowels with silent *e*.

✓ Tell if *-es*, *-s*, or *-ed* endings describe past or present action.

Comprehension

✓ Reread for details.

✓ Use a KWL Chart.

✓ Preview a story.

✓ Use a Details Chart.

✓ Tell fantasy from reality.

✓ Use a Fantasy and Reality Chart.

Grammar and Writing

✓ Identify plural nouns.

✓ Identify common nouns and proper nouns.

✓ Identify subject and object pronouns.

✓ Write a how-to article.

✓ Write a descriptive paragraph.

✓ Write about an event.

Self-Evaluation Questions

- What do you really understand about the ways animals care for their young?

- What questions do you still have?

- What grade do you deserve for your effort? Why?

57

UNIT 2

Powerful
Forces of Nature

Thunder and lightning! Floods! Hurricanes and tornadoes! Erupting volcanoes! Powerful forces of nature change our world.

READINGS

1

Vesuvius Erupts!

2

Hurricane!

3

Thunder and Lightning

The Big Question

How do people protect themselves from powerful forces of nature?

LISTENING AND SPEAKING

Get ready! In this unit, you will discuss the powerful forces of nature and what to do in an emergency.

WRITING

When a big storm comes, people need to stay inside. You will write a how-to article that explains a game people can play.

Bonus Reading

Lost and Found: Mountain Climbers

Quick Write

Which selection do you think will be the most interesting? Write your reasons.

What Do You Know about Forces of Nature?

Words to Know

1. Use these words to talk about the forces of nature.

 sunny

 snowy

 cloudy

 rainy

 windy

 foggy

---

2. What's the weather like today?

Today is _____ .

 sunny

 snowy

 rainy

 windy

 cloudy

 foggy

3. What can happen if there is too much weather?

If it is too _____ , we could have _____ .

a flood

a drought

a tornado

a blizzard   *or*   an avalanche

4. Use these words to talk about other forces in nature.

hail   tsunami   earthquake

Your Stories about Forces of Nature

Missouri, U.S.A.

Dominican Republic

Jennifer

I live in Missouri. There are many tornadoes in this part of the country. Sometimes I have to leave my house to go to a shelter. Once a tornado blew the roof off our house. My family was fine because we went to a shelter.

Alberto

I live in the Dominican Republic. My country is part of an island in the Caribbean Sea. Almost every year the island is hit by powerful hurricanes. They can destroy the houses that people live in. We are always prepared for this kind of emergency.

Japan

Bangladesh

Atsuo

I live near Japan's highest mountain. Mount Fuji is more than 12,300 feet high. It is a dormant volcano. That means the volcano is not active. Artists paint beautiful pictures of Mount Fuji. But I can look at a real sleeping volcano every day.

Bani

We have many floods in Bangladesh. In the spring, the snow on the mountains melts. We also have lots of rainstorms in my country. This means our rivers often fill with too much water. The floods destroy towns and crops.

What about you?

1 What kind of weather do you have where you live?

2 How are these students' stories similar to yours?

3 Do you have other stories about forces of nature? Tell your story!

Vocabulary

Vesuvius Erupts!

Vesuvius Erupts! is about a volcano that erupted almost 2,000 years ago.

Words in Context

A **volcano** is a mountain that is formed when gases, ash, and lava push up from the earth. The gases build up inside the earth. Sometimes they erupt, or burst, through the crater. The **crater** is the opening of a volcano. An **eruption** causes lava and ash to fly out of the crater. **Lava** is melted rock. **Ash** is lava that has been ground into small pieces. The lava and ash from an eruption can cause damage.

Key Words

- volcano
- ash
- lava
- crater
- eruption

Mount St. Helens is a volcano in Washington State. Its last large eruption was in 1980.

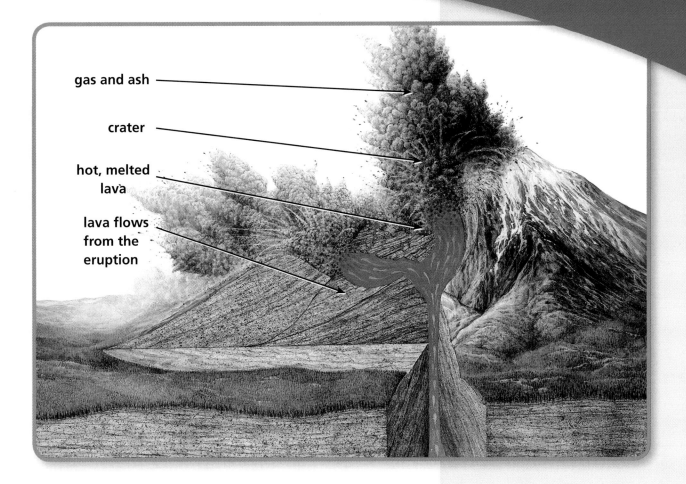

gas and ash

crater

hot, melted lava

lava flows from the eruption

Practice

Practice

Use each key word in a sentence.

Make Connections

An eruption happens suddenly. Do you remember something that happened very suddenly? How did you feel? What did you do?

Academic Words

similar
almost the same, but not exactly

evidence
proof

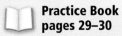

Practice Book
pages 29–30

NARRATIVE TEXT

Social Studies

The Big Question

How does learning about dangerous forces of nature in the past help us know what to do today?

Reading Strategy

Make Predictions

- Read the title.
- Look at the illustrations and photos. Read the captions.
- Read the date at the beginning of the story.
- Predict what this story will be about.

Vesuvius Erupts!

The Temple of Isis was in Pompeii.

Pompeii was a city on the Bay of Naples.

POMPEII, A.C.E. 79

It was a very hot morning in Pompeii. Even Mount Vesuvius gave no shade to the city below.

Hot weather did not stop the people of Pompeii. They walked in the streets and shopped in the markets. The smell of bread from a bakery filled the air. Musicians played and sang for the shoppers.

At a restaurant, two women ordered food. A man tied his dog to a tree. Just then, the ground began to shake. The dog barked. It was scared.

---

shade dark area that gets little sun or light

Pompeii was a busy town.

Check Up > When does this story take place?

People stopped talking. The women looked worried. Was it an earthquake?

Boom! Suddenly, the top of Mount Vesuvius blew off! Now the mountain had a crater. The volcano was erupting. Fire and huge black clouds rose into the sky. The ground started to shake. People ran from their homes.

Ash and smoke covered the sun. Daytime turned into darkness. Lava poured down the mountain. Hot ash and rocks fell from the sky.

The ash covered people's heads, faces, and bodies. It burned their eyes. It filled their mouths as they called for help. The air became very thick with ash and gases. It was hard to breathe.

The ash piled higher and higher. Soon, it blocked the streets. Roofs collapsed because the ash was so heavy. The ash filled the rooms. Pompeii was disappearing. Soon, the ash buried the city.

The House of the Great Fountain was found in Pompeii.

This is a wall painting in Pompeii of the goddess Flora.

---

earthquake   sudden shaking of the earth

collapsed   fell down

About 2,000 people stayed in the city. Some chose to stay. Others were trapped. All of them died. But 20,000 people were able to escape.

In less than two days, ash and rocks buried the city. Heavy rain made the ash hard like cement. Pompeii stayed buried for almost 1,700 years!

In about 1750, the King of Naples ordered workers to uncover Pompeii. They started to dig through the rocks. They found the city almost exactly as it was when the volcano erupted.

Workers still dig in the ruins of Pompeii.

The eruption of Vesuvius was a tragic event. But it also helped us learn about life long ago. Many people and objects were frozen in time. As a result, today we know much about how people lived almost 2,000 years ago.

---

tragic   sad

Practice Book pages 31–32

Reading Strategy

Make Predictions

Before reading, you predicted what the story would be about.

- Were your predictions correct?
- Did making predictions help you to understand the story? How?

Think It Over

1 Where does the story take place?

2 What were people in Pompeii doing the day Vesuvius erupted?

3 What was the first sign of danger?

4 Why did it take so long to discover Pompeii?

Vesuvius and Pompeii

▲ Aerial photo

This aerial photo of the crater was taken from an airplane.

▲ Burned bread

Workers found 81 loaves of bread.

▲ Roman city

Pompeii is in Italy. The people who lived on these narrow streets were Romans.

▲ Victims

Many of the victims were farmers. The soil on Vesuvius was very rich. The farmers were not afraid of the volcano. It had been quiet for years!

▲ Bay of Naples

Vesuvius is on the coast of the Bay of Naples.

▲ Ruins

Today, people from all over the world visit the ruins at Pompeii.

Activity to Do!

These two pages told you about Pompeii.

- Choose another city.
- Research that city online or in the library.
- Create two pages, using pictures and words, to tell about that city.

Word Analysis & Fluency

Word Analysis

Ending: -ed

The words in red below name actions that happened in the past. They end in -ed.

Present	Past
The ice cubes **melt** today. ⟶	The ice cubes **melted** yesterday.
The dogs **bark** today. ⟶	The dogs **barked** yesterday.

Adding the -ed ending to **melt** adds a syllable.

Adding the -ed ending to **bark** does not add a syllable.

Rule Box

If the letter *t* or the letter *d* comes before the -ed ending, then -ed is pronounced as a separate syllable.

Practice

Work with a partner. Take turns.

melted	stayed
filled	decided
started	waited
called	helped

1. Copy the words.

2. Circle the word if the -ed adds another syllable.

3. Cross out the word if the -ed does not add another syllable.

4. List other words that end in -ed. Have your partner tell if the -ed adds another syllable.

Practice Book

page 33

72

Fluency

Look Ahead

Sometimes readers look for hard words before they read. Then they try to figure them out.

Practice

| Pick one passage. | → | Find any hard words. | → | Practice saying those words. | → | Read the passage aloud. |

1. It was a normal day in Pompeii. Then Mount Vesuvius erupted. The volcano sent hot ash and rocks into the sky. Soon the town was buried. The people who stayed in the city died.

2. At a restaurant, two women ordered food. A man tied his dog to a tree. Just then, the ground began to shake. The dog barked. He was scared.

   People stopped talking. The women looked worried. Was it another earthquake? Boom! Suddenly, the top of Mount Vesuvius blew off!

3. In less than two days, ash and rocks buried the city. Heavy rain made the ash hard like cement. Pompeii stayed buried for almost 1,700 years!

   In about 1750, the King of Naples ordered workers to uncover Pompeii. They started to dig through the rocks. They found the city almost exactly as it was when the volcano erupted.

Comprehension

Sequence of Events

In many stories, events happen in a certain order. This order is called the **sequence** of events.

Learning Strategy

Retell

Retell the selection to a partner.

 Ask your partner to respond to the Big Question for this reading.

Practice

Read this series of events from *Vesuvius Erupts!* List the events in the order in which they happened.

   a. Pompeii stayed buried for hundreds of years.

   b. Vesuvius erupted.

   c. People in Pompeii started an ordinary day.

   d. Piles of ash covered the town.

   e. Rain made the ash hard as cement.

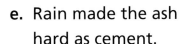

📖 **Practice Book page 34**

Use a Plot Diagram

A Plot Diagram can help you summarize the main events in a story in the order they happened.

Practice

Answer the questions below to complete the plot diagram.

1. Which event would you add to the middle of the diagram?
   a. Women talked at a restaurant.
   b. Pompeii was buried by ash in less than two days.
   c. The king of Naples gave an order.
   d. People shopped in outdoor markets.

2. Which sentence could be added to the end of the diagram?
   a. Workers began to uncover Pompeii.
   b. About 2,000 people stayed in town.
   c. Huge black clouds blocked the sun.
   d. Two women ordered snacks.

3. Which events in the diagram took place in 79 A.C.E.? List them.

4. Use what you know to describe Pompeii today.

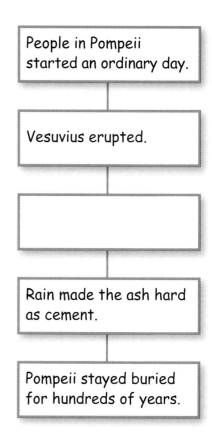

People in Pompeii started an ordinary day.

Vesuvius erupted.

Rain made the ash hard as cement.

Pompeii stayed buried for hundreds of years.

Extension

Suppose you wanted people in the future to know about your life. Get five items that tell about your life. Share the items with your class. Tell why you chose them.

Grammar & Writing

Action Verbs

As you read about the eruption of Vesuvius, you could almost see the action of that day. The action words are verbs. A **verb** describes what the subject of a sentence did. The action verbs below are in red.

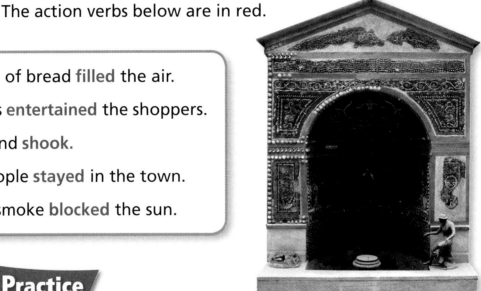

> The smell of bread **filled** the air.
>
> Musicians **entertained** the shoppers.
>
> The ground **shook**.
>
> Many people **stayed** in the town.
>
> Ash and smoke **blocked** the sun.

Practice

Read each sentence. Write the action verb.

1. A man tied his dog to a tree.

2. The dog barked.

3. People ran from their homes.

4. Hot ash covered people's heads, faces, and bodies.

5. Fire jumped from the top of the volcano.

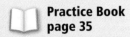

Practice Book page 35

Write a Review

As you read *Vesuvius Erupts!* were you interested in the story? What parts did you like the most? Was there any part you did not like? Read Jason's reaction to the story.

At first, I did not want to read "Vesuvius Erupts!" I did not know what Vesuvius was. I never heard of Pompeii. Then, I read the story. I thought about that hot day. I imagined I was there. I fell when the earth shook. I smelled the fire on the mountain. I heard the dog bark. I saw the ash fall like snow. But it was not nice like snow. The ash was hot and it hurt. It was hard to breathe after the eruption. If I lived near a volcano, I would be afraid. The story made me think. Now, I want to read more about volcanoes.

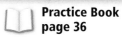

SPELLING TIP

Regular verbs that tell about actions in the past end in *-ed*. Make sure you add *-ed* to regular verbs when you write about the past.

📖 **Practice Book page 36**

Practice

Write your reaction to *Vesuvius Erupts!* What did you like or dislike? What would you tell someone else about this story?

Writing Checklist

✓ Did you use action verbs? Circle them.

✓ Did you spell regular past-tense verbs with the *-ed* ending?

✓ Can a partner understand what you wrote?

Vocabulary

Hurricane! is a story about a family on vacation who lived through a hurricane.

Words in Context

Key Words

- **breeze**
- **hurricane**
- **shelter**
- **lightning**
- **thunder**

① A **breeze** is a light wind. When it is breezy, plants and trees may move a little.

② A **hurricane** is a big tropical storm. It brings very strong winds and a large amount of rain.

3 When a hurricane is coming, people can go to a **shelter**. A shelter is a place where people are protected from forces of nature.

4 **Lightning** is a flash of light in the sky. It happens during a storm. It is usually followed by a loud sound called **thunder.**

Academic Words

major
big or important

region
large land area

Practice

Use each key word in a sentence.

Make Connections

What was the biggest storm you ever lived through?

📖 **Practice Book**
pages 37–38

LITERATURE

Realistic Fiction

The **Big** Question

Why is it important to know about dangerous weather?

Reading Strategy

Visualize Setting

The setting of this story is important. As you read *Hurricane!*, picture each new setting in your mind.

- How is the setting important to the story?

HURRICANE!

by Tracey Baptiste
illustrated by Amy Huntington

On our second day of vacation, I splashed in the sea. Mom and Dad sat on the shore. It was sunny, but not for long.

A man ran toward us. He worked at a nearby hotel.

"Señor! Señorita!" he called. "A big storm is coming. You must leave the beach now!" He told us that a hurricane was approaching. Everyone had to go to a shelter.

---

approaching   moving nearer

"But the water is so nice," I said sadly.

"Hurricanes are dangerous. We must leave," Dad said.

Mom smiled to make me feel better. Just then, I felt a breeze. Suddenly, the wind grew stronger. Sand flew into my face.

"Let's go!" Dad said.

Check Up How does the beach change before the storm?

81

Mom and I packed all of our bags. Dad nailed wood over the windows of the beach house. This would protect the house from wind and rain.

"Our vacation is ruined," I cried.

"Maybe the storm won't last for long," Mom said. "But we can't take chances. We have to go where it is safe."

"We'll be OK," said Dad. "Think of this as an adventure."

I tried to cheer up. I might have an exciting story to tell my friends. But soon my adventure did not seem so fun.

The hurricane came closer. Lightning flashed! Thunder clapped! Rain fell from the sky. It was hard to see out the car windows.

---

protect   shield from danger

ruined   spoiled or destroyed

"The streets will flood soon," Dad said.

"We must drive carefully," Mom said.

The shore was pounded by angry waves. The waves were strong and high. It was the afternoon, but the sky was as dark as night.

People on the coast were leaving their homes. The roads were crowded with cars. Our car moved slowly down the wet road.

---

coast where the land meets the ocean

Check Up Describe the setting on the road.

Later that day, we stopped at a hotel. Usually, people on vacation stayed there. Now it was a shelter for travelers. Many people were in the lobby of the hotel. They were caught by the storm. They had nowhere else to go.

Mom and I watched the news on TV. The weather forecaster talked about the storm. She explained that soon it would be over. But some people were trapped. They were caught by the fast storm.

But my family was warm and safe inside the shelter. Outside, the wind and rain shook the trees and windows. People who were still outside needed help.

---

forecaster   person who tells what the weather will be like

trapped   not able to get out

One news reporter was in a boat. He saw a family on a raft. Their house was flooded, but they were fine. Emergency teams rescued these people. By that night, everyone was safe. I was happy now. And I had a story to share.

---

flooded covered in water

rescued helped or saved

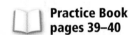
Practice Book pages 39–40

Reading Strategy

Visualize Setting

- Describe some part of the setting in your own words.
- Could this story have happened where you live? Why or why not?
- Did visualizing the setting help you to understand the story? How?

Think It Over

1 What was the first sign of the hurricane?

2 What was the family's drive to the shelter like?

3 How did the narrator feel when he was inside the shelter?

4 Do you think being in a hurricane is an adventure? Why or why not?

Phonics & Fluency

Phonics

Digraphs: *ch, sh, th*

Sometimes two letters combine to make one sound. The letters *ch*, *sh*, and *th* are examples. These letters can come anywhere in a word.

ch	sh	th
chances	share	think
cheer	shelter	this
approaching	shore	thunder
watched	flash	weather
beach	splashed	with

Practice

Work with a partner. Take turns.

1. Choose a word from the chart. Say the word aloud.
2. Without looking at the word, have your partner tell whether the word has the letters *ch*, *sh*, or *th*.
3. List six more words that are spelled with *ch*, *sh*, or *th*.

Fluency
Read for Speed and Accuracy

You should read quickly. But never read so quickly that you lose your understanding.

Practice

| Read for one minute. | → | Count the words you read. | → | Study any hard words. | → | Read and count again. |

The shore was pounded by angry waves. The waves were	10
strong and high. It was the afternoon, but the sky was as dark	23
as night.	25
People on the coast were leaving their homes. The roads were	36
crowded with cars. Our car moved slowly down the wet road.	47
Later that day, we stopped at a hotel. Usually, people on	58
vacation stayed there. Now it was a shelter for travelers. Many	69
people were in the lobby of the hotel. They were caught by the	87
storm. They had nowhere else to go.	89
Mom and I watched the news on TV. The weather forecaster	100
talked about the storm. She explained that soon it would be	111
over. But some people were trapped. They were caught by the	122
fast storm.	124
But my family was warm and safe inside the shelter. Outside,	135
the wind and rain shook the trees and windows. People who	146
were still outside needed help.	151
One news reporter was in a boat. He saw a family on a raft.	165
Their house was flooded, but they were fine. Emergency teams	175
rescued these people. By that night, everyone was safe. I was	186
happy now. And I had a story to share.	195

Comprehension

Clues to Setting

To understand a story better, it helps to form a picture in your mind of the setting. The **setting** is where and when a story takes place. The setting of *Hurricane!* is near the beach during a hurricane.

Learning Strategy

Retell

Retell the story to a partner.

 Ask your partner to respond to the Big Question for this reading.

Practice

Work with a partner. Look for clues to the setting.

• Reread pages 80–81.

• Copy the words, phrases, or sentences that help you get a clear picture of the setting of the story.

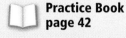 **Practice Book page 42**

Use a Word Web

A Word Web helps you create a picture using just words.

Practice

Copy and complete this Word Web to describe the setting of _Hurricane!_

1. Read the questions in each circle.

2. Write in each circle what you visualize, or picture, in your mind.

3. Compare your Word Web with your partner's. How are they alike? How are they different?

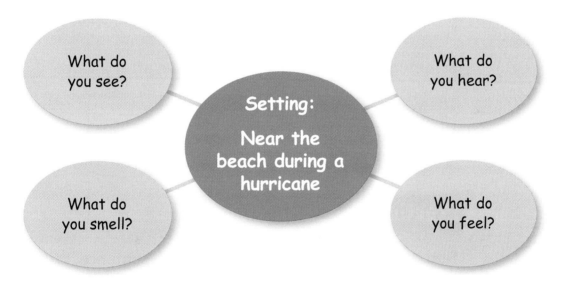

What do you see?

What do you hear?

Setting:

Near the beach during a hurricane

What do you smell?

What do you feel?

Extension

A setting can be drawn or even built in a model. Think of a setting that you know well. Picture how it might look during a big storm. Bring your setting to life in a description, drawing, or model. Share your setting with your class.

Grammar & Writing

Adjectives and Noun Phrases

Nouns name persons, places, or things. **Adjectives** help readers picture a noun. The adjective often comes right before the noun. Together the adjective and the noun form a **noun phrase**.

Noun	Adjective	Noun Phrase
breeze	strong	strong breeze
story	exciting	exciting story
waves	angry	angry waves

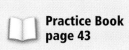
Practice Book page 43

Sometimes, writers place the adjective after a verb.

The water is warm.
Hurricanes are dangerous.
The streets were flooded.

Practice

Find the noun and the adjective in each sentence. Write the adjective before the noun to form a noun phrase.

Sentence	Noun Phrase
The breeze was soft.	the soft breeze

1. The sea is calm.
2. The sky was gray.
3. The fish is big.

4. The lobsters were red.
5. The wind is fierce.
6. The damage was great.

Write a Descriptive Paragraph

A good writer uses words that help the reader picture a scene. Noun phrases help make a scene come alive.

As you read Sven's descriptive paragraph, picture what he is describing. What nouns and adjectives did Sven combine to make noun phrases?

I looked out the window of our old log cabin. I could not see the gray boathouse. I knew it was at the end of the stone path. I saw it just five minutes before. But now the thick fog hid it! I could not see my wooden rowboat, either. It was little, but I loved that boat. I hoped it was safe. Now I had to wait until this terrible storm passed. When I heard the wind, I jumped in surprise. The wind broke the window.

SPELLING TIP

The letters for *c*, *k*, and *ck* all have the /k/ sound.

looked   cabin
walkway   thick
covered   crack

Use a dictionary to learn which letters spell the /k/ sound.

Practice Book page 44

Practice

Picture a time when the weather was strange or amazing. Write a paragraph to describe that scene. Use noun phrases to help you.

Writing Checklist

✔ Did you use noun phrases?

✔ Did you proofread your writing to make sure your spelling is correct?

✔ Can a partner understand your description?

Vocabulary

You will read three passages about thunder and lightning. Each passage gives information in a different format.

Words in Context

A **bolt** of lightning looks like a white line in the sky.

Key Words

- bolt
- electricity
- temperature
- evaporate

Electricity is a kind of energy. Lightning in the sky is electricity.

Which of these three pictures show items that use electicity? ▼

Temperature is a measure of how hot or cold something is.

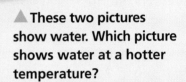
▲ These two pictures show water. Which picture shows water at a hotter temperature?

When water gets hot, it boils. Then, water will **evaporate** and change into a vapor or gas.

Practice

Use each key word in a sentence.

Make Connections

How does thunder and lightning make you feel?

Academic Words

conduct

carry; allow electricity to pass through it

security

protection from harm or loss; safety

 Practice Book pages 45–46

INFORMATIONAL TEXT

Internet Article

The **Big** Question

What can you do to keep safe during thunder and lightning storms?

Reading Strategy

Identify Genre

- A **genre** is a type of writing. Stories, poems, articles, plays, and letters are just some of the genres that we use.

- What do you notice about the genres of the passages that follow?

Thunder and Lightning

Electricity in the Sky

Lightning is a big flash of electricity. It is released during a storm. Lightning strikes more often in the summer than in the winter. That's because there are more storms in the summer. Sunny weather and hot temperature heat the air and make water evaporate. The hot air and water vapor rise into the sky. As they rise, they meet the cold air.

---

flash   sudden, bright light

vapor   small drops that float in the air

Cloud to cloud lightning

Up in the Clouds

The cold air makes the water vapor turn back into water droplets or ice crystals. That forms a cloud. Inside the cloud, the droplets and crystals carry a tiny bit of electricity. The electricity builds until lightning suddenly forms.

Lightning can jump from one cloud to another (see image 1). It can move from a cloud to the ground (see image 2). Sometimes lightning can even move from the ground up to a cloud (see image 3).

Cloud to ground lightning

Lightning is five times hotter than the sun. Lightning heats the air around it so quickly that the air explodes. Thunder is the noise we hear when the air explodes.

Catch Me If You Can!

Light moves faster than sound. This means we see the flash of lightning before we hear the thunder. It takes five seconds for the noise of the thunder to go one mile. If you see lightning and then hear thunder five seconds later, the storm is one mile away. If thunder comes ten seconds after lightning, the storm is two miles away.

Ground to cloud lightning

---

droplets   very small drops of liquid

crystals   little pieces of ice

Check Up   How do you know this is an informational article?

95

Staying Safe
in a Lightning Storm

Lightning can be dangerous.
Here are some tips to stay safe.

Outdoors

1. Check if thunderstorms are in the forecast.
2. Find shelter in a strong building or in a car with a hard roof.
3. Do not stand under trees that are alone in the middle of a field.
   Do not stand under tall trees when there are shorter trees close by.
4. Do not stand near things that are made of metal.

Indoors

1. Close all the windows and doors.
2. Do not use the telephone.
3. Do not take a bath or shower. Stay away from water.
4. Turn off electrical appliances, including computers and TVs.

The Lightning Crouch

If you feel your skin tingle or your hair stand up, this could mean you are about to be hit by lightning. Get into the "Lightning Crouch." Crouch down low and curl into a small ball. Put your hands on your knees, and keep your head down. Try to be as small as you can, with very little touching the ground. DO NOT LIE ON THE GROUND!

---

forecast   description of what is likely to happen in the future

November 12, 2010

Dear Grandma,

Thank you for your letter. I am sorry you had a bad day. Maybe it will make you feel better to know about Roy C. Sullivan. I just read about some bad luck he had. He was struck by lightning more times than anyone else in the world! From 1942 to 1977, he was struck seven different times by lightning!

Roy worked in a national park. He was standing on a high tower in the park when the first lightning bolt hit him. Years later, he was driving along a road when lightning struck him again. Lightning hit him five more times.

Roy was unlucky, but he was also lucky. It's very dangerous to be struck by lightning. He was never badly hurt, though.

You and I can be even luckier than Roy. At school I learned how to protect myself from being struck by lightning. I'll tell you how in my next letter.

Love,
Emilio

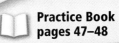

Practice Book pages 47–48

Reading Strategy

Identify Genre

- What features let you know that you were reading different genres?
- How was reading Emilio's letter different from reading the Internet article?

Think It Over

1. Why don't we hear thunder at the same time we see lightning?

2. Where is a good place to go during a lightning storm?

3. Describe the Lightning Crouch.

4. Why is Roy C. Sullivan unusual?

Word Analysis & Fluency

Word Analysis

Word Parts

As you read, look for little words that are part of big words. Some bigger words are made of two little words put together.

lightning   outdoors

Practice

Work with a partner. Each of you should copy the words below.

- Circle all of the little words you see.
- Compare your list to your partner's. Did you find the same words?
- Add other big words that contain little words to your list.

thunderstorm	lookout	dangerous
anyone	anywhere	hotter

Fluency

Read with Expression

When you read aloud, use your voice to show feelings.

Practice

| Read silently. | ▷ | Read aloud. | ▷ | Get comments. | ▷ | Read aloud again. |

Thank you for your letter. I am sorry you had a bad day. Maybe it will make you feel better to know about Roy C. Sullivan. I just read about some bad luck he had. He was struck by lightning more times than anyone else in the world! From 1942 to 1977, he was struck seven different times by lightning!

Roy C. Sullivan worked in a national park. He was standing on a high tower in the park when the first lightning bolt hit him. Years later, he was driving along a road when lightning struck him again. Lightning hit him five more times.

Extension

Choose a kind of dangerous weather, like heavy rain, thick fog, a heat wave, or extreme cold. Research safety rules that would help protect people in that kind of extreme weather. Give a presentation to help others learn how to stay safe.

Comprehension

Compare Genres

Genres have different purposes and are organized in different ways.

Informational Articles are usually organized into paragraphs and have a title and headings. An article often has photographs or illustrations to make the facts clearer.

How-To Posters often have headings and numbered steps. The headings help you find information. The numbered steps tell the order you should follow.

Friendly Letters have a date, a salutation (Dear Grandma), a message, and a closing (Love, Emilio).

Learning Strategy

Take Notes

Take notes on the selection.

Share your notes with a partner.

Ask your partner to respond to the Big Question for this reading.

November 12, 2010

Dear Grandma,
Thank you for your letter. I am sorry you had a bad day. Maybe it will make you feel better to know about Roy C. Sullivan. I just read about some bad luck he had. He was struck by lightning more times than anyone else in the world! From 1942 to 1977, he was struck seven different times by lightning!
Roy worked in a national park. He was standing on a high tower in the park when the first lightning bolt hit him. Years later, he was driving along a road when lightning struck him again. Lightning hit him five more times.
Roy was unlucky, but he was also lucky. It's very dangerous to be struck by lightning. He was never badly hurt, though.
You and I can be even luckier than Roy. At school I learned how to protect myself from being struck by lightning. I'll tell you how in my next letter.

Love,
Emilio

Practice

Copy the chart. Write "article," "poster," or "letter" in the final column." There can be more than one answer.

Statements	Genre
1. **Purpose**: It is written to one person.	letter
2. **Purpose**: It is written to present information to many people.	
3. **Headings**: It has headings.	
4. **Numbered Steps**: It has steps that tell what order to follow.	
5. **Information**: It tells facts.	

Practice Book

page 50

100

Use a Venn Diagram

A **Venn Diagram** makes it easy to see what is the same or different about two items. Circle A represents one item. Circle B represents another. The part that overlaps represents things that are true for both.

Practice

Create a Venn diagram to compare two of the genres. Use the statements from the chart on the previous page.

- Choose two of the three genres from the selection.
- Draw a blank Venn diagram. List one genre in Circle A. List the other genre in Circle B.
- Write any statements that are true for one genre, but not for the other genre, in the big parts of Circle A or Circle B.
- Write any statements that both genres have in common in the section labeled *Both*.

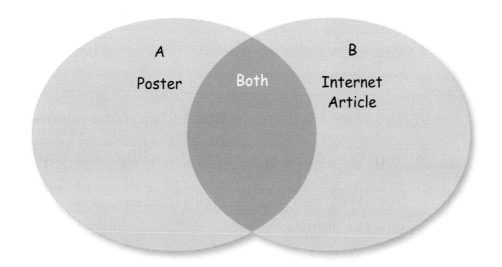

Grammar & Writing

Commands

A **command** gives an order or makes a request.
Commands usually state an action that needs to be done.

Rules	Examples
A command usually starts with a verb.	*Close all the windows and doors.*
Add a name if you want to call attention to one person.	*Steve, close all the windows and doors.*
Form negative commands with the helping verb **do** + **not**. You can also use a contraction **don't**.	*Do not use the telephone.* *Don't use the telephone.*
End a command with a period or an exclamation point for emphasis.	*Do not lie on the ground!*

Practice

Read each sentence. Express what is described as a command. Write the command.

1. You want to tell people to find shelter before the storm starts.

2. You want everyone to stop talking for a minute.

3. You want Alissa to turn on the news.

4. You want your friend to run inside because you saw lightning.

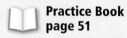
Practice Book page 51

Write a How-To Article

In a how-to article, the author explains a process step by step. The author gives instructions or commands to follow.

- The verbs are in the command form.
- The instructions are short and clear.
- All the steps are in order.

Read Katrinka's instructions for finding a lost pet.

1. Walk in the area where your pet was last seen and call its name.
2. Get something familiar to your pet, like a blanket, or toy.
3. Leave the item where your pet was last seen. Your pet may come back to that familiar smell.
4. Call your local Animal Control Officer. Report your missing pet.
5. Create posters with your pet's picture. The poster should also contain an adult's phone number.
6. Put your posters all around your town.

SPELLING TIP

Word parts like -*ly* and -*y* form a new word:

    quick/quickly
    cloud/cloudy

Use a dictionary to learn how word parts change a word's meaning.

Practice Book page 52

Practice

Write your own how-to article to explain the rules of a game.

- List any materials needed to play the game.
- Explain the steps players take to play the game.
- Check to make sure the steps are in the right order.
- Try it out with a partner! Make sure you didn't miss a step.

Writing Checklist

✔ Are your verbs in the command form?

✔ Are your instructions short and clear?

✔ Can a partner follow your steps?

LOST AND FOUND: Mountain Climbers

Many people like to climb Mount Hood in Oregon. Mount Hood is a beautiful mountain. But it can be dangerous.

Mount Hood often has sudden storms. People can start climbing in nice weather. Then they may be trapped in a snow storm. How do rescue teams find lost climbers?

Many mountain climbers carry tools to help them. One tool is a cell phone. Lost climbers can call for help.

Another tool is a Global Positioning System, or GPS. A GPS shows climbers where they are. Rescue teams find the climbers if they need help.

A GPS works with signals from satellites.

A GPS is very useful for climbers.

A GPS works with satellites that orbit, or circle, Earth. Satellites send signals to Earth. The GPS picks up the signals to show people where they are on Earth.

Some climbers also carry a Mountain Locator Unit, or MLU. An MLU sends out a radio signal. If climbers get lost, they turn on the MLU. A rescue team picks up the signal. Then the team finds the climbers.

Mountain climbers need to be careful. They should pay attention to the weather. They should carry tools in case they get lost. Then they can enjoy their climb.

The Big Question

How do people protect themselves from powerful forces of nature?

Written	Oral	Visual/Active
Safety Guidelines	**Interview**	**World Map**
Write school guidelines for students to follow during a tornado or hurricane.	Interview someone who saw some extreme weather. Record your interview.	Create a map of the world. Post photos on it showing types of extreme weather that are found around the world.
News Article	**Folk Tale**	**Graphic Organizer**
Research on the Internet to find a place that recently had severe weather. Write a newspaper article about the events.	Long ago, people created folk tales to explain the weather. Tell your own folk tale to explain a form of extreme weather.	You learned about different types of lightning. Research and create a graphic organizer to show other types of weather, like rain, clouds, or storms.
Adventure Story	**Vocabulary Hunt**	**Board Game**
Imagine that you survived the most terrible storm! Write an adventure to tell your story.	Listen to daily weather reports for one week. Record as many weather words as you can. Create a collage to express the feelings of those words.	Create a game called Storm Survivor. Use slides for bad weather and ladders for survival techniques. Create cards to add weather events.

✔ Learning Checklist

Word Analysis and Phonics

✔ Tell whether -ed adds a syllable to a word.

✔ Read words in which ch, sh, or th stand for one sound.

✔ Identify little words that are part of bigger words.

Comprehension

✔ List a sequence of events.

✔ Use a Plot Diagram.

✔ Identify clues to setting.

✔ Use a Word Web.

✔ Compare genres.

✔ Create a Venn Diagram.

Grammar and Writing

✔ Identify action verbs.

✔ Recognize and use adjectives and noun phrases.

✔ Recognize and use commands.

✔ Write a review of a reading.

✔ Write a descriptive paragraph.

✔ Write a how-to article.

Self-Evaluation Questions

- How did what you learned connect with other learning?

- Were you proud of anything you did? What was it?

- Were you disappointed by anything you did? How could you improve next time?

107

UNIT 3
Telling Tales

Everyone enjoys a good story. You will read a poem, a tale, a play, and a legend. They are all different genres, or types, of literature. What stories do you like to tell or read?

READINGS

My Museum Friend

Why Mosquitoes Buzz in People's Ears

The Shoemakers and the Elves

The Big Question

?

What do the characters in tales have in common?

LISTENING AND SPEAKING

What stories do you like? You will talk about your favorite stories.

WRITING

You will make up some characters and tell a tale about them.

Quick Write

If you told a story about your life, what genre would you choose? Write your thoughts.

Bonus Reading

John Henry and the Machine

What Do You Know about Telling Tales ?

Words to Know

1. Use these words to talk about reading.

 magazine

 newspaper

 recipe

 cereal box

 website

 directions

---

2. What do you read?

I read _____ .

 a recipe

 a cereal box

 a website

 a newspaper

 a magazine

 directions

110

3. What happens when you read?

When I read a _____ , I _____ .

see photographs *and* **illustrations**

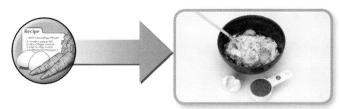

measure ingredients

get information

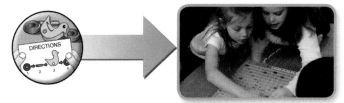

learn the rules

4. Use these words to talk about other things to read.

poster

envelope

encyclopedia

map

Your Stories about Telling Tales

Oklahoma, U.S.A.

Raymond

I live in Oklahoma. My father told me a tale about the first strawberries. He said they were made to help two friends who were angry with each other. When they shared the fruit, they became friends again. Now, I always share my strawberries.

David

I live in the United Kingdom. My house is near the National History Museum. I like to visit the fossil of a giant dinosaur. We call him Claws. My favorite poem is *Bones to Stones*. It is about a dinosaur just like Claws.

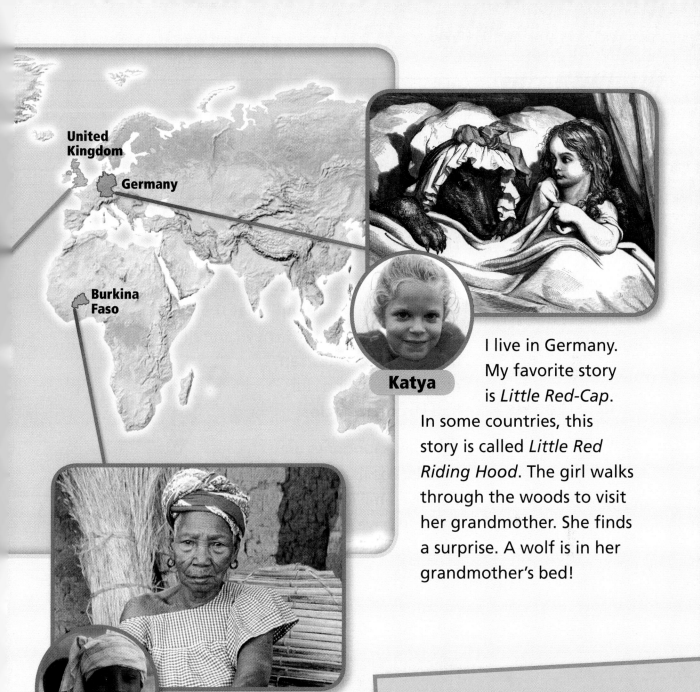

United Kingdom

Germany

Burkina Faso

Katya

I live in Germany. My favorite story is *Little Red-Cap*. In some countries, this story is called *Little Red Riding Hood*. The girl walks through the woods to visit her grandmother. She finds a surprise. A wolf is in her grandmother's bed!

Bacia

I am from Burkina Faso. The summers in Africa are hot and rainy. That means there are lots of mosquitoes. My grandmother tells a story about mosquitoes that buzz in people's ears.

What about you?

1 Do any of these stories sound familiar to you? Which ones?

2 How are these students' stories similar to yours?

3 Do you have other stories or tales? Tell your story!

My Museum
Friend

Vocabulary

My Museum Friend is a poem about a dinosaur in a museum.

Words in Context

Key Words

dinosaur

muscles

fossils

sandstone

species

extinct

1 This **dinosaur** lived millions of years ago. Scientists can figure out what the dinosaur looked like when it was alive. They can tell how big a dinosaur was. They can also tell that dinosaurs had strong **muscles**.

2 Dinosaur bones are **fossils**. Fossils are things that lived millions of years ago and have turned to rock. Fossils of dinosaur footprints are often found in **sandstone**. Sandstone is a kind of rock.

3 A **species** is a group of plants or animals that are all similar. If every plant or animal in a species dies, the species becomes **extinct**. Dinosaurs are extinct. The blue whale is one animal that could become extinct if people do not protect it.

◀ Today, the extinct passenger pigeon is found only in museums.

Practice

Use each key word in a sentence.

Make Connections

What are some of your favorite wild animals? How would you feel if any of those animals became extinct?

Academic Words

locate
find

link
connection

📖 **Practice Book**
pages 55–56

LITERATURE

Poetry

The **Big** Question

Could a dinosaur be a character?

Reading Strategy

Identify Characters

- Read the poem.
- Identify the characters in the poem.

My Museum Friend

by Kathleen Hughes

illustrated by Elizabeth Allen

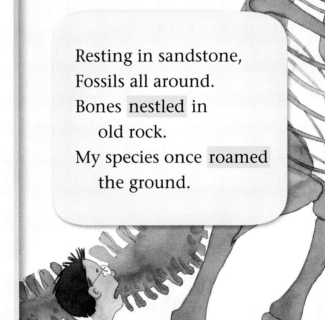

Resting in sandstone,
Fossils all around.
Bones nestled in
    old rock.
My species once roamed
    the ground.

---

nestled   rested close to someone or something

roamed   went from place to place without a plan

116

Wondering about my muscles?
Or my powerful legs that are so strong?
I was Dinosaur, king of all the land.
How did everything go wrong?

Extinct! That's what I am to you.
My whole world went haywire.
Like a puff of smoke I disappeared
Because of ice, an asteroid, or fire.

Goodbye, my friend.
It looks like your visit has ended today.
It's been great chatting with you.
For now, I have nothing else to say.

---

haywire   working in a completely wrong way

chatting   talking in a friendly way

Practice Book
pages 57–58

Reading Strategy

Identify Characters

- Who are the characters? How do you know?

- Did identifying the characters help you understand the poem? How?

Think It Over

1 What is this poem about?

2 Who is the narrator of this poem?

3 How did the dinosaur become extinct?

117

Dinosaurs

Asteroid ▶

Many scientists think dinosaurs became extinct after an asteroid hit Earth. An asteroid is a large rock in the sky.

▲ Pterodactyl

This is a fossil of a flying dinosaur. The pterodactyl was one of the first animals to fly.

▲ From earth to museum

Diggers uncover a dinosaur bone in the ground. They will send the bone to a museum.

118

▲ Helpful tools

Scientists use many tools to find and dig up fossils.

▲ Tyrannosaurus rex

The tyrannosaurus rex was one of the largest dinosaurs. It had very sharp teeth.

▲ Footprints

Dinosaur footprints are millions of years old. They are found all over the world.

▲ Triceratops

This is the skull of a triceratops. This dinosaur had three horns.

Activity to Do!

These two pages use pictures and words to tell you about dinosaurs.

- Choose a dinosaur you like.
- Research that dinosaur.
- Create two pages about that dinosaur. Use pictures and words.

Word Analysis & Fluency

Word Analysis

Synonyms and Antonyms

Notice the words in red. What do they mean?

> Wondering about my muscles?
> Or my powerful legs that are so strong?

The words *powerful* and *strong* both mean "having great power or strength." They are synonyms. **Synonyms** are words that mean the same or almost the same thing.

The word *weak* means "not having strength or power." *Weak* and *strong* are antonyms. **Antonyms** are words that have opposite meanings.

Practice

Work with a partner. Replace each underlined word with a synonym or an antonym from the box.

1. I'd love to <u>chat</u> more.

2. Were you <u>weak</u>?

3. Where did you <u>wander</u>?

4. Can we chat again <u>now</u>?

later	roam
strong	talk

Practice
Book

page 59

120

Fluency

Read with Expression

When you read aloud, use your voice to show feelings.

Practice

Read silently.	Read aloud.	Get comments.	Read aloud again.

Wondering about my muscles?
Or my powerful legs that are so strong?
I was Dinosaur, king of all the land.
How did everything go wrong?

Extinct! That's what I am to you.
My whole world went haywire.
Like a puff of smoke I disappeared
Because of ice, an asteroid, or fire.

Goodbye, my friend.
It looks like your visit has ended today.
It's been great chatting with you.
For now, I have nothing else to say.

Comprehension

Character

Characters are the people or animals in a story or a poem. The main characters are the most important ones. The minor characters are less important.

Learning Strategy

Retell

Retell the poem to a partner.

 Ask your partner to respond to the Big Question for this reading.

Practice

Make a list of all the characters you can remember from each of these fairy tales. Circle the main characters.

1. Cinderella

2. Little Red Riding Hood

3. Goldilocks and the Three Bears

4. The Three Little Pigs

Practice Book page 60

Use a Character Web

A Character Web can help you organize information about characters in a story or a poem.

Practice

Copy this Character Web. Use it to show what you know about the dinosaur in *My Museum Friend*.

- Complete your web with information from the poem.
- Share your web with a partner.
- Discuss why it is useful to know more about a main character.

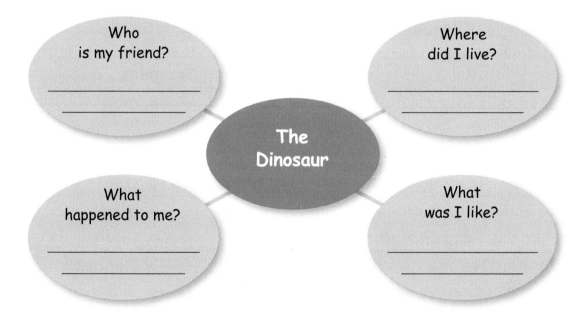

Extension

Where have you seen a dinosaur?
Make a drawing or model of a dinosaur.
Share it with your class.

Grammar & Writing

Regular Past-Tense Verbs

Past-tense verbs name actions that already happened. The verbs in red are in the past tense.

> Dinosaurs once **roamed** the land.
>
> They **disappeared** a long time ago.

The verbs *roam* and *disappear* are both regular verbs. Regular verbs add *-ed* to form the past tense.

Rules	Examples	
For most verbs, add *-ed*.	roam	⟶ roam**ed**
	disappear	⟶ disappear**ed**
For verbs ending in *-e*, drop the *e* and add *-ed*.	like	⟶ lik**ed**
	save	⟶ sav**ed**
For verbs ending in a consonant and *y*, change the *y* to *i* and add *-ed*.	try	⟶ tr**ied**
	study	⟶ stud**ied**
For verbs that have one vowel and end with one consonant, double the consonant and add *-ed*.	plan	⟶ plan**ned**
	skip	⟶ skip**ped**

Practice

Write the past-tense form of each verb.

1. dry
2. remove
3. show
4. clap
5. chase
6. hunt
7. grab
8. carry

Practice Book page 61

124

Write a Song

One way to write words for a song is to use a tune you know. Think about the tune. Tap out the rhythm. Match new words to the rhythm. Karume used the rhythm of *I've Been Workin' on the Railroad* to write this song.

> I've been talking with a dinosaur.
> My friends all said, "No way!"
> Yes, I've been talking with a dinosaur
> And it had a lot to say.
>
> It talked about its mighty muscles,
> Its legs and tail so strong.
> It said it was the royal leader.
> Until everything went wrong.

Practice

Write your own song.

- Choose a subject. It could be dinosaurs or anything else.
- Tap the rhythm of a song you know.
- Write some words about your subject.
- Match the words to the rhythm of the song. The song gives you a frame for writing.

SPELLING TIP

The letter pairs *ch*, *sh*, and *th* all say one sound. These pairs can appear anywhere in a word:

chin	march
shine	marsh
thing	with

Practice Book page 62

Writing Checklist

✓ Did the words work with the song you chose?

✓ Did you use past-tense verbs correctly?

✓ Can you sing your song to a partner?

125

Why Mosquitoes Buzz in People's Ears

Vocabulary

Why Mosquitoes Buzz in People's Ears is a pourquoi tale. It explains why mosquitoes can't talk.

Key Words

tidbit

mischief

nonsense

duty

satisfied

council

Words in Context

1 Sasha and Pedro put a **tidbit** of food in the fish tank.

2 My little brother is always getting into **mischief**.

3 Jessie likes to whisper **nonsense** in Kevin's ear.

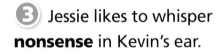

4 Every citizen has a **duty** to vote. Voting helps cities and towns make plans.

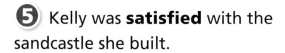

5 Kelly was **satisfied** with the sandcastle she built.

6 This student **council** meets once a week. It is the school's government.

Practice

Use each key word in a sentence.

Make Connections

What are your duties at home?
What is a student's duty at school?

Academic Words

emerge

appear or come out from somewhere

transmit

send or pass

Practice Book pages 63–64

127

The Big Question

How are animal characters like people?

Reading Strategy

Identify Sequence of Events

- Pay attention to the order in which events happen.
- Notice how one action leads to another action.

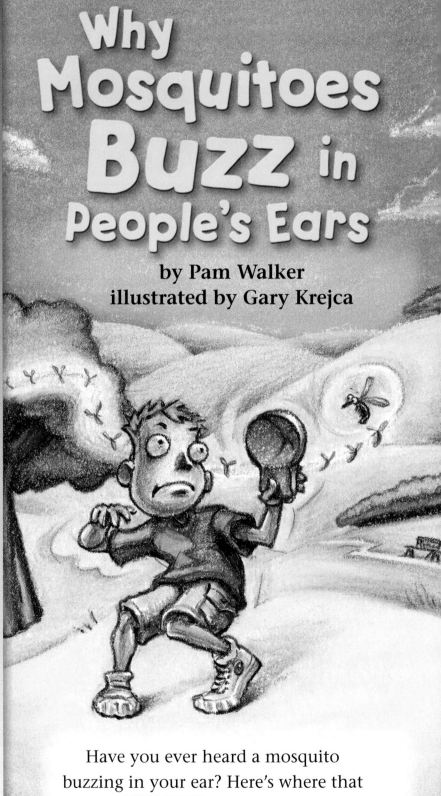

Why Mosquitoes Buzz in People's Ears

by Pam Walker
illustrated by Gary Krejca

Have you ever heard a mosquito buzzing in your ear? Here's where that insect's annoying habit came from.

---

annoying   making you feel a little angry

One summer day, Mosquito saw Turtle sunbathing on a rock.

He flew over to his friend and whispered in her ear. "I have a tidbit of news!"

"You should not gossip," said Turtle.

"But wait until you hear this!" said Mosquito. "Farmer grew a carrot as large as an elephant!"

"That is nonsense!" Turtle cried. "I don't want to hear it!" She stuffed leaves in her ears and walked away.

Snake was in a tree branch when Turtle walked by.

"Hi, Turtle!" he hissed. "It'sssss me." But Turtle could not hear him.

---

gossip   talk about someone in a way that is not nice

CheckUp   **What did Turtle do after Mosquito started to gossip?**

"Turtle must be mad at me," Snake thought sadly. He slithered out of the tree to hide under a log. Mouse lived in the log. When she saw Snake coming, she ran from her home.

"What's wrong?" Rabbit asked the timid mouse.

"I have no time to talk," said Mouse. "Run! Danger!"

So Rabbit ran as fast as she could. "Run!" she cried. "Danger!"

Monkey heard Rabbit's cries. "Something bad is happening!" he thought. "It is my duty to tell the others!"

He jumped from tree to tree. "Run!" he called. "Danger!"

---

slithered   smoothly moved from side to side across a surface

timid   shy or scared

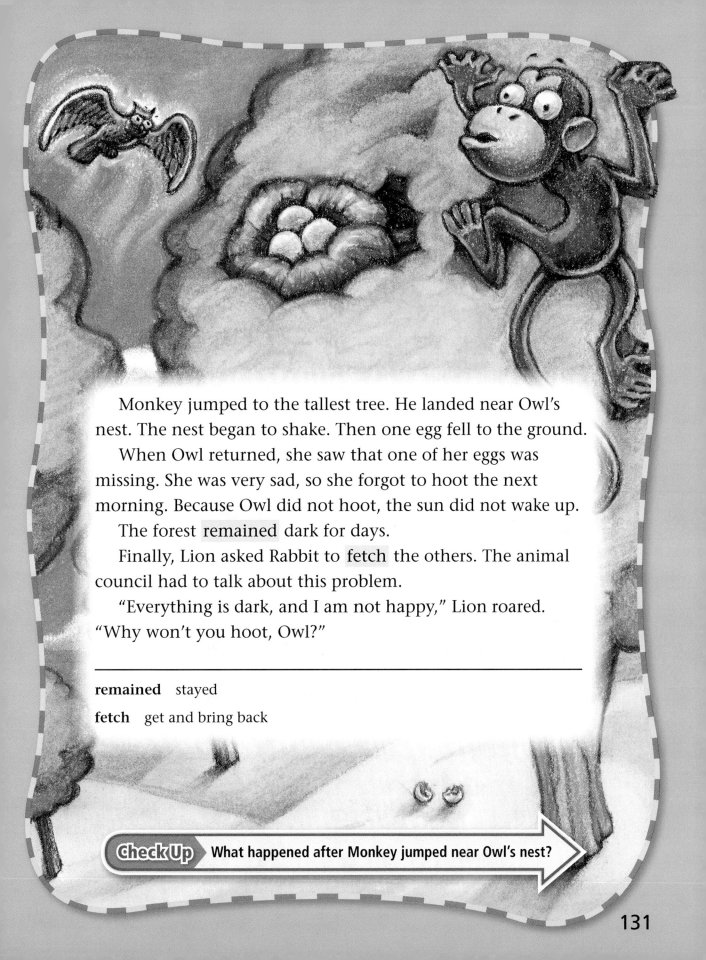

Monkey jumped to the tallest tree. He landed near Owl's nest. The nest began to shake. Then one egg fell to the ground.

When Owl returned, she saw that one of her eggs was missing. She was very sad, so she forgot to hoot the next morning. Because Owl did not hoot, the sun did not wake up.

The forest remained dark for days.

Finally, Lion asked Rabbit to fetch the others. The animal council had to talk about this problem.

"Everything is dark, and I am not happy," Lion roared. "Why won't you hoot, Owl?"

---

remained   stayed

fetch   get and bring back

CheckUp What happened after Monkey jumped near Owl's nest?

131

"I am too sad to hoot," said Owl. "Monkey broke one of my eggs!"

Lion looked at Monkey. "Rabbit said there was danger!" said Monkey. "I wanted to warn everyone!"

Lion looked at Rabbit. "Mouse told me to run!" Rabbit said.

Lion looked at Mouse. "Snake came to my house! I was afraid he would eat me!" cried Mouse.

"I wassss not hungry. I was sssssad," hissed Snake. "Turtle would not sssssspeak to me."

Just then, Turtle walked by.

"Turtle!" Lion roared. "Are you Snake's friend?"

"What?" Turtle removed the leaves from her ears. "Yes, I am Snake's friend."

---

warn   tell someone that something bad or dangerous may happen

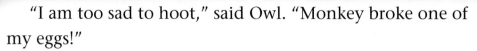

132

"Then why didn't you speak when Snake said hello?" asked Lion.

"I did not hear him," said Turtle. "Mosquito gossips, so I put leaves in my ears."

"All this mischief started with you, Mosquito," the angry lion said. "You may never talk again."

All the animals were satisfied, but not Mosquito. Even today mosquitoes want to talk. But all they can do is buzzzzz!

📖 **Practice Book pages 65–66**

Reading Strategy

Identify Sequence of Events

- What action started the events of the story?
- Did identifying the sequence of events help you understand the story? How?

Think It Over

1. Why doesn't Turtle want to hear Mosquito's words?

2. Why does Snake think Turtle is mad at him?

3. Who decides that the animal council must meet?

4. Why does Lion tell Mosquito never to talk again?

133

Phonics & Fluency

Phonics

Long Vowel Pairs

Long vowel sounds can be spelled with two vowels together making a pair.

Long Vowel Pairs				
Long *a*	**Long *e***	**Long *i***	**Long *o***	**Long *u***
wait, day	bean, tree	cried	roam, toes	true, fruit

Did you notice that each word has two vowels together? Which vowel do you hear? Which vowel is silent?

Rule Box

When two vowels are together, the first vowel is usually long, and the second vowel is silent.

w a i t   t r e e   t r u e

Practice

Write the word that has the vowel sound.

road	skies	clue	fail	need

1. long *a* _____

2. long *e* _____

3. long *i* _____

4. long *o* _____

5. long *u* _____

Fluency

Look Ahead

Sometimes readers look for hard words before they read. They then try to figure them out.

| Pick one passage. | Find any hard words. | Practice saying those words. | Read the passage aloud. |

1 Mosquito likes to make mischief. One day, Mosquito's gossip leads to big problems for all the animals.

2 "You should not gossip," said Turtle.

"But wait until you hear this!" said Mosquito. "Farmer grew a carrot as large as an elephant!"

"That is nonsense!" Turtle cried. "I don't want to hear it!" She stuffed leaves in her ears and walked away.

Snake was in a tree branch when Turtle walked by.

3 Then one egg fell to the ground.

When Owl returned, she saw that one of her eggs was missing. She was very sad, so she forgot to hoot the next morning. Because owl did not hoot, the sun did not wake up.

The forest remained dark for days.

Finally, Lion asked Rabbit to fetch the others. The animal council had to talk about this problem.

Comprehension

Sequence of Events

In many stories, events happen in a certain order. That order is called the **sequence**.

Outline

Make an outline of the main characters and events in the story.

Share your outline with a partner.

? Ask your partner to respond to the Big Question for this reading.

Practice

Read these events from *Why Mosquitoes Buzz in People's Ears*. List them in order.

- Turtle told Mosquito that Mosquito should not gossip.
- Turtle stuffed leaves in her ears and walked away.
- Mosquito flew over to tell Turtle some news.
- Mosquito whispered some gossip in Turtle's ear anyway.
- Mosquito saw Turtle sunbathing on a rock.

 Practice Book page 68

136

Use a Sequence of Events Chart

A Sequence of Events Chart helps you put story events in the correct order. Start with the first event. Then write each event that happens after that. Finish with the last event.

Practice

Copy and complete this chart.

- Reread the story. List the tale's events in the correct order.
- Share your chart with a partner.
- Discuss what would happen if someone read the events in the wrong order.

Sequence of Events in *Why Mosquitoes Buzz in People's Ears*	
First	Mosquito sees Turtle sunbathing.
Next	
Next	
Next	Owl forgets to hoot.
Next	
Next	
Last	Lion tells Mosquito he can never talk again.

Extension

Do you know how to play Telephone? Form a circle with your classmates. The first person whispers a sentence to the next person. That person whispers the same sentence to the next person. The last person says the sentence aloud. Did the message change? How?

Grammar & Writing

Irregular Past-Tense Verbs

You cannot form the past tense of **irregular verbs** by adding -*ed* to the end of the word.

> One summer day, Mosquito **saw** Turtle sunbathing on a rock. He **flew** over to his friend and whispered in her ear.

Saw is the past-tense form of the verb **see**.
Flew is the past-tense form of the verb **fly**.

This chart shows some other irregular past-tense verbs.

Present tense	Past tense
come	came
grow	grew
fall	fell

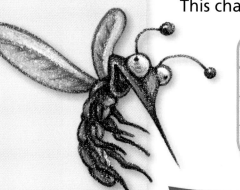

Practice

Write the past-tense form of the underlined verb.

1. Turtle <u>grows</u> tired of Mosquito's silly stories.

2. Turtle <u>says</u> she does not like gossip.

3. Snake <u>thinks</u> Turtle must be mad at him.

4. Mouse <u>sees</u> Snake near her house.

5. Mouse, Rabbit, and Monkey <u>run</u> away from Snake.

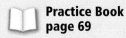
Practice Book page 69

138

Write a Tale

A **tale** is a story about imaginary events. Some tales have magical characters, like fairies and elves. In Meghan's tale, the characters are animals. Pay attention to each character. You will learn about them from their words and actions.

Raccoon was very upset. He was stuck in a tunnel and needed help. So he called and called. Finally, the other animals came.

Fox laughed when he saw what was wrong. "You're too big to go snooping in someone else's tunnel," he said.

Beaver sat quietly and thought. Squirrel chattered and looked for nuts. Rabbit hopped around with excitement. Then Beaver said, "We must dig." That was all.

The animals dug around Raccoon. Fox just watched them work. They dug until the dirt flew into the sky. Finally, the hole was big enough for Raccoon to come out.

"Thank you," he said to all the animals.

Fox said, "You will never go snooping again!"

SPELLING TIP

In a notebook, write words you have trouble spelling. Study the words until they become easier to spell.

Practice Book page 70

Practice

Write your own tale.

- Choose some characters.
- Decide what each character is like.
- Write a fun tale about those characters.

Writing Checklist

✓ Did your tale have a beginning, a middle, and an end?

✓ Did you spell your verbs correctly?

✓ Can a partner get to know at least one character?

Vocabulary

The Shoemakers and the Elves is a play about two elves and two shoemakers who help each other.

Words in Context

1 The queen wore her **fine** clothing when her picture was painted.

2 Taxis quickly **whisk** riders across town.

3 Many red **stitches** hold this baseball together.

Key Words

- **fine**
- **whisk**
- **stitches**
- **stroke**
- **bare**
- **wink**

④ At the **stroke** of midnight, Cinderella ran out of the palace.

⑤ Old Mother Hubbard's cupboard was **bare.** There was no food inside.

⑥ How much time does it take you to **wink** an eye?

Practice

Use each key word in a sentence.

Make Connections

"In the wink of an eye" means "very quickly." People use that expression even when something does not happen as quickly as winking. What are some expressions you use?

Academic Words

voluntary
done without expecting payment or reward

---

appreciate
be grateful for

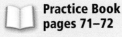

**Practice Book
pages 71–72**

LITERATURE

Play

Reading Strategy

Infer and Predict

- As you read, make inferences. Think about what you already know that the text doesn't tell you.

- As you read, make predictions. Try to predict what will happen next.

The Shoemakers and the Elves

by Amanda Hong
illustrated by Sheila Bailey

Cast

Pixie, a female elf

Lumkin, a male elf

Amelia, a shoemaker and Diego's wife

Diego, a shoemaker and Amelia's husband

Scene 1: Two elves are looking into the window of a house. Two elderly shoemakers are inside. They are yawning. The elves wear tattered clothing. They are cold.

Lumkin: Let's play a trick on them!

Pixie: No, Lumkin. I think we have had enough fun for one day. We need a warm place to rest.

Lumkin: You're right. I don't want to get chased out of another house. I'm cold.

Pixie: [She looks in the window again.] Those people look tired.

Lumkin: And their shelves look bare. The shoemakers have nothing to sell.

Pixie: They're talking. Let's listen.

---

elderly old

tattered old and torn

Check Up   Why do you think Lumkin and Pixie were chased out of a house?

143

[The shoemakers are tired and worried. Tools for tomorrow's work are on a table.]

Diego: I don't know how we can survive. We have no more leather to make shoes.

Amelia: What will we do?

Diego: Maybe we should close our shop.

Amelia: Then what will we do? Sell firewood?

Diego: Why not? I can chop down the walls to find wood.

[They yawn as they walk upstairs.]

Amelia: Let's sleep. We'll think about this tomorrow.

[The elves enter the shoemakers' shop.]

Pixie: This is sad, Lumkin.

---

survive stay alive

Lumkin: Yes, I am very sad. There is no bread here for us to eat.

Pixie: I think the shoemakers' problems are bigger than ours. We should help these people.

Lumkin: He wants firewood. Let's chop up the house!

Pixie: No tricks, Lumkin.

Lumkin: We could finish making the shoes. Then tomorrow the shoemakers will get a big surprise.

Pixie: Yes! We will make so many beautiful shoes. Everyone will want to buy them.

Lumkin: If you get that cheese on the mousetrap, I will make the shoes as quick as a wink.

Pixie: You always ask me to do the hard things.

---

mousetrap   trap that uses food to catch mice

CheckUp   Why does Lumkin want cheese from the mousetrap?

[The elves finish working.]

Lumkin: Let's put away the tools and leather.

Pixie: Whisk the mess away. Let's go play!

[The elves leave. The next morning, the shoemakers come downstairs. They find the new shoes. They are speechless.]

Amelia: Look, Diego! Shoes! I must be dreaming!

Diego: Did you get up and work last night?

Amelia: No! I was going to ask you the same thing!

Diego: Then I must be dreaming, too! These shoes are beautiful.

Amelia: Look at these stitches! The quality is very fine.

Diego: Even we could not have made such special shoes.

Amelia: Let's put them in the window.

[They embrace.]

---

speechless   unable to speak

quality   degree to which something is good or bad

146

[One week later, the shoemakers sit at the table.]

Diego: We are very lucky. Every night, someone makes shoes for us.

Amelia: And every day, we sell all those new shoes. We have so many customers now.

Diego: Who do you think is making the shoes, Amelia?

Amelia: I have no idea, Diego. But I would like to thank them. Wouldn't you?

Diego: Yes. But how?

Amelia: I have an idea!

[That night, Diego and Amelia do not go to bed. Instead, they hide behind a curtain. At the stroke of midnight, the two elves appear at the window.]

Diego: [whispering] Elves?

Amelia: [whispering] Elves! How delightful!

---

customers   people who buy goods and services

delightful   very nice

CheckUp Do you think Amelia and Diego are happy to see the elves? Why?

[The clock rings twelve times. Lumkin and Pixie sneak into the house through the window.]

Pixie: Try to be quiet, Lumkin. We do not want to wake up the people.

[Lumkin runs to the mousetrap. He grabs the bait and eats it.]

Pixie: That cheese is for mice.

Lumkin: It's for hungry elves, too. I like to eat before I work.

Pixie: Well, there is a lot of work to do tonight.

[The elves go to the table and begin working. The shoemakers watch from behind the curtain.]

Amelia: We should do something nice for those hard workers.

Diego: I have an idea!

---

sneak   go somewhere very quietly so as not to be seen or heard

bait   food that is used to attract animals so you can catch them

[The next night, the shoemakers put two packages on the table. Then they hide and peek through the curtains.]

Lumkin: It's midnight.

Pixie: That means it's time to go to work.

[The elves look around. The table is bare except for the gifts.]

Lumkin: Where is the leather? Where are the tools?

Pixie: What is this?

[The elves open the packages.]

Pixie: These beautiful things are for us!

[They try on the clothes and shoes. Then they dance with joy.]

Lumkin: Let's go outside and play!

Pixie: But what about our work?

Lumkin and Pixie: Ha ha!

[The elves laugh as they dance. The shoemakers smile as the happy elves leave.]

peek look secretly at something that you are not supposed to see

📖 **Practice Book pages 73–74**

Reading Strategy

Infer and Predict

- What time did the elves come?
- How can you make that inference?

Think It Over

1 What problem do Amelia and Diego have?

2 What do the elves want when they go to the shoemakers' house?

3 How do the elves and the shoemakers help each other?

4 If you were the shoemaker, what would you do to help the elves?

Phonics & Fluency

Phonics

Vowel Pair *ea*

Each word below has the vowel pair *ea*. Read the words.

Vowel Pair *ea*	
Long *e*	**Short *e***
eat	bread
each	head
speak	ready

Rule Box

The vowel pair *ea* can have two sounds: the long *e* sound, as in ***eat,*** or the short *e* sound, as in ***bread***. If you see a word you do not know, try saying the *ea* sound both ways.

Practice

Read the sentences with a partner. Take turns.

- Pixie and Lumkin sneak into the shop.
- They eat cheese instead of bread.
- They make nice shoes from leather.
- Amelia thinks she is dreaming.

Practice Book

📖

page 75

1. List the words in which *ea* has the long *e* sound.

2. Then list the words in which *ea* has the short *e* sound.

Fluency

Read for Speed and Accuracy

You should read quickly. But never read so quickly that you lose your understanding.

Practice

| Read for one minute. | Count the words you read. | Study any hard words. | Read and count again. |

[Lumkin and Pixie sneak into the house through the window.]	10
Pixie: Try to be quiet, Lumkin. We do not want to wake up	23
the people.	25
[Lumkin runs to the mousetrap. He grabs the bait and eats it.]	37
Pixie: That cheese is for mice.	43
Lumkin: It's for hungry elves, too. I like to eat before I work.	56
Pixie: Well, there is a lot of work to do tonight.	67
[The elves go to the table and begin working. The shoemakers	78
watch from behind the curtain.]	83
Amelia: We should do something nice for those hard workers.	93
Diego: I have an idea!	98
[The next night, the shoemakers put two packages on the	108
table. Then they hide and peek through the curtains.]	117
Lumkin: It's midnight.	120
Pixie: That means it's time to go to work.	129
[The elves look around. The table is bare except for the gifts.]	141
Lumkin: Where is the leather? Where are the tools?	150
Pixie: What is this?	154
[The elves open the packages.]	159
Pixie: These beautiful things are for us!	166

Comprehension

Infer and Predict

To **infer** is to figure out something that the author doesn't directly tell you. To **predict** is to make guesses about what will happen.

Learning Strategy

Retell

Retell the story to a partner.

 Ask your partner to respond to the Big Question for this reading.

Practice

Make inferences or predictions about the passage.

> The manager hired Manuel instead of Joe. He needed an experienced waiter, and he did not have time to teach Joe everything. Joe hoped to find a job soon. Summer vacation had already started. School would begin again in September. There were lots of "Help Wanted" signs on Main Street. Joe would keep looking for a job.

1. Has Joe been a waiter before?

2. Has Manuel been a waiter before?

3. Is Joe a student?

4. Will Joe return to school soon?

5. Does Joe want a job?

6. Will Joe get a job?

 Practice Book page 76

Use an Infer and Predict Chart

An Infer and Predict Chart helps you answer questions about a story or play.

Practice

Work with a partner. Read the dialogue in the first column.

- Discuss what you know about the elves and the shoemakers.
- Answer the questions in the second column.

Dialogue	Infer/Predict
Lumkin: Let's play a trick on them! **Pixie:** No, Lumkin. I think we have had enough fun for one day. We need a warm place to rest. **Lumkin:** You're right. I don't want to get chased out of another house. I'm cold.	**1. Infer:** Which elf seems more sensible? **2. Infer:** Have the elves been chased out of a house before?
Lumkin: If you get that cheese on the mousetrap, I will make the shoes as quick as a wink. **Pixie:** You always ask me to do the hard things.	**3. Predict:** What will Lumkin and Pixie do with the cheese? **4. Infer:** Which does Pixie think is harder, getting cheese or making shoes?
Pixie: These beautiful things are for us! **Lumkin:** Let's go outside and play! **Pixie:** But what about our work? **Lumkin and Pixie:** Ha ha!	**5. Infer:** Do the elves like their gifts? **6. Predict:** Will Lumkin and Pixie come back to work after they play?

Extension

Think of a time when you helped someone. Make a drawing that shows what you did. Share it with your class.

153

Grammar & Writing

The Verb *Have*

Have means to own or possess.

> **Diego:** We **have** no more leather to make shoes.
> **Amelia:** I **have** an idea!

This chart shows how to use **have** with different subjects. Notice that the verb is in the present tense.

Subject	Form of *have*
Amelia, Diego	has
he, she, it	has
elves, shoemakers	have
I, you, we, they	have

Practice

Write each sentence. Use the correct present-tense form of *have*.

1. The shoemakers _____ a problem.

2. Pixie tells Lumkin that she _____ a desire to help.

3. The elves _____ an idea.

4. Together, they _____ excellent skills as shoemakers.

Practice Book
page 77

Write a Skit

A **skit** is a short scene from a play. Trevor wrote this skit about mysterious nighttime events. As you read, think about how a skit is different from other kinds of stories.

What Happened Last Night?

Cast: Mr. Bear, Mrs. Bear, Bertie Bear, 6, Baby Bear, 2

[Scene: Outside the Bears' house. It is early morning.]

Mr. Bear: What's this? My fishing rods are in the trees!

Mrs. Bear: Who would do that? We are friends with all the animals.

Bertie: Someone took the wheels off my trucks! How can I play with my toys?

Mrs. Bear: I should check my sculpture. [She goes inside.] Oh, no! There is a hat on its head! My art is not a hat rack!

Baby Bear: [crying] Where is my teddy bear?

Bertie: [searching] Here it is, Baby. It was hidden under a chair.

Baby Bear: [points to the ground] What's that?

Mr. Bear: It's a footprint. It's shaped like a shoe.

Everyone: Humans! Run inside! They'll eat our porridge!

Practice

Write your own skit! Include this information:

- the cast
- the scene
- the dialogue
- stage directions

Writing Checklist

✔ Did your skit tell a story?

✔ Did you write a cast list and a description of the scene?

✔ Can a partner understand your skit?

John Henry and the Machine

by Michael Dunn Moriarty
illustrated by Nicole Laizure

The world is full of stories about the mighty John Henry. But he started out as a baby, just like the rest of us. The only difference was that even as a baby, John Henry could lift a sledgehammer over his head.

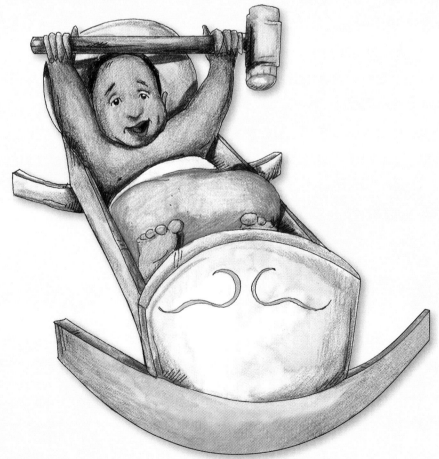

156

Young John Henry loved that big hammer. He liked to pound on rocks. Up went the hammer, and then down it came. John Henry could turn big rocks into dust.

When he grew up, John Henry worked for the railroad. He was bigger and stronger than everybody else on the job. All day long, he hammered steel spikes into rocks. He broke every rock that was in the way of the railroad.

John Henry was as happy as a man could be. Then a stranger brought a new machine to town.

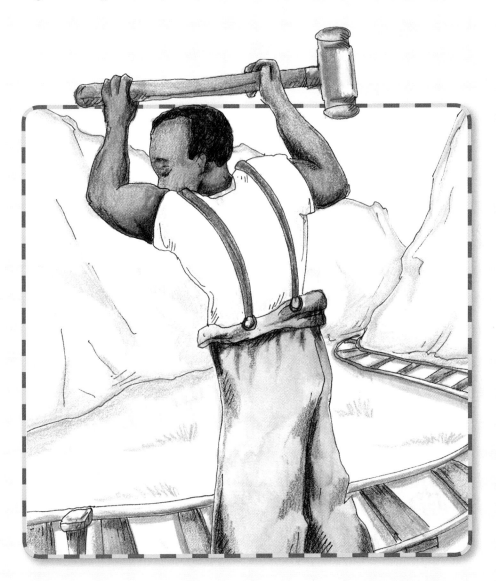

The stranger boasted that his drilling machine could do more work than ten men.

"Impossible!" John Henry cried. "No machine can do more work than I can."

The stranger challenged John Henry to a contest. He wanted to prove what his machine could do.

He pointed to a wall of rock. "Let's see who can drill through that!" Then he started his machine. John Henry raised his hammer.

John Henry and the machine worked. They worked all day and all night. They each broke through the thick wall, one rock at a time.

The next morning, dust and people were everywhere. A crowd had gathered to watch the contest. They came to cheer for John Henry.

By noon, the stranger's machine began to sputter. But John Henry was still going strong.

Suddenly, the machine hissed. Then it died. John Henry brought his hammer down for one final blow.

When the dust cleared, everyone saw that John Henry had broken through the rock wall!

"You won the contest!" they cried.

John Henry smiled. "Yes, I did," he said. "Now, I just want to get back to work."

UNIT 3 Wrap Up

The Big Question

What do the characters in tales have in common?

Written	**Oral**	**Visual/Active**
Character Sketch	**20 Questions**	**Book Cover**
Choose your favorite character from the selections. Describe the character. Tell why the character is your favorite.	With a partner, play 20 Questions. Choose a character from the unit. Your partner must ask you questions to try to identify the character.	Make a book cover for one of the selections. Include the main character or characters on your cover.
Newspaper Article	**Pourquoi Tale**	**Character Cards**
Rewrite one of the selections as a newspaper article. Have the characters explain why they did the things they did.	Make up your own pourquoi tale. Tell it to a group of classmates. Be sure to include a strong character.	Create a set of picture cards for some of the characters you've read about. Draw pictures like the ones in your book, or use your own ideas.
Mixed-Up Tale	**Act It Out**	**Character Charades**
Choose one selection. Write a new version of the story. Include a character from one of the other selections.	Work with a group to perform *The Shoemakers and the Elves* for your classmates.	Play charades with a small group. Act out a character from the unit. Others must guess who your character is.

160

✓ Learning Checklist

Word Analysis and Phonics

✓ Identify synonyms and antonyms.

✓ Read words with vowel pairs that spell long vowel sounds.

✓ Recognize the vowel pair *ea* and identify when it spells the long e and short e sounds.

Comprehension

✓ Identify characters.

✓ Use a Character Web.

✓ Put events in sequence.

✓ Use a Sequence of Events Chart.

✓ Make inferences and predictions.

✓ Use an Infer and Predict Chart.

Grammar and Writing

✓ Identify regular past-tense verbs.

✓ Identify irregular past-tense verbs.

✓ Use the verb *have* correctly.

✓ Write a song.

✓ Write a tale.

✓ Write a skit.

Self-Evaluation Questions

- What questions do you have about what you've learned?

- What follow-up work do you need to do?

- How has what you've learned changed your thinking?

161

UNIT 4
Problem Solvers

An empty building can become a problem. So can an unwanted plant or a broken machine. You will read nonfiction articles about people working to solve problems.

READINGS

1

New Life for Old Buildings

2

Running for Office

3

Problems Stop London Eye

The Big Question

How do people solve problems?

LISTENING AND SPEAKING

Different problems will have different solutions. You will talk about ways to solve problems.

WRITING

Do you like to eat in restaurants? You will write a paragraph that compares two restaurants.

Bonus Reading

The Trouble with Kudzu

Quick Write

What are some important problems in your town? Write about one of them.

What Do You Know about Problem Solvers ?

Words to Know

1. Use these words to talk about solving problems.

 petition

 brainstorm

 research

 debate

 investigate

 design

2. Whom can you ask to help solve a problem?

I can ask _____.

 a paramedic

 an architect

 a detective

 a guidance counselor

 a politician

 an inventor

3. How can people solve problems?

The _____ can _____ to solve a problem.

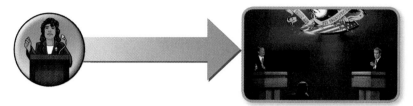

debate

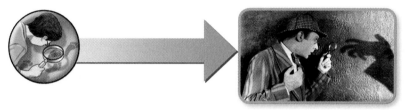

investigate

design

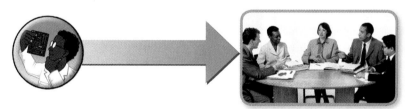

brainstorm

Your Stories about Problem Solvers

the Netherlands

South Korea

Brian

I live in the Netherlands. Some of our parks have mazes made of hedges. There is only one correct path through a maze. I enter at one end and exit at the other. It's fun to get lost in a maze.

Suna

In South Korea people love to play Go. It is an old Chinese board game. You try to circle the other player's stones with your own. It's not easy, but it's fun!

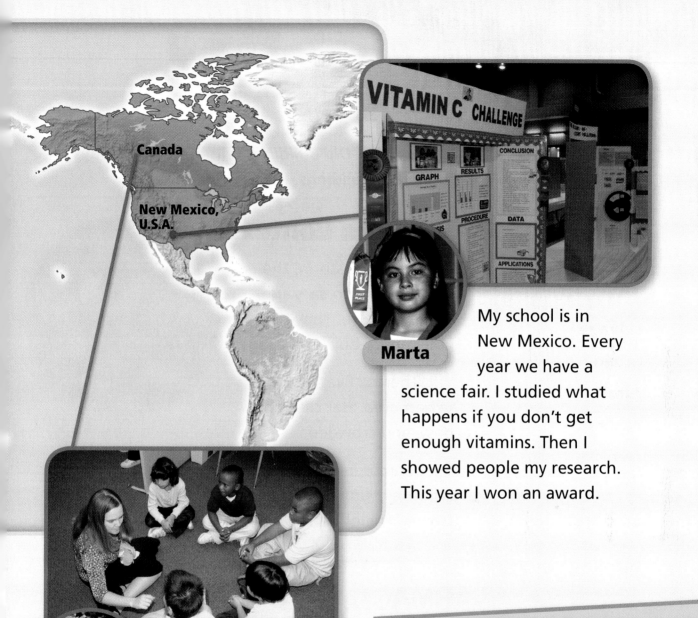

Canada

New Mexico, U.S.A.

Marta

My school is in New Mexico. Every year we have a science fair. I studied what happens if you don't get enough vitamins. Then I showed people my research. This year I won an award.

Arnoud

I live in Canada. My school has a new program. It teaches students to solve problems without fighting. I learn special skills, such as how to listen to others. I also learn to say what I feel without getting angry.

What about you?

1 What problems have you solved?

2 How are these students' stories similar to yours?

3 Do you know other stories about solving problems? Tell your story!

167

New Life for
**OLD
BUILDINGS**

Vocabulary

New Life for Old Buildings tells about new ways to use old buildings.

Words in Context

1 After the storm, the women tried to **salvage** their furniture. They did not want to buy new things.

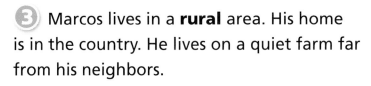

2 Theresa lives in an **urban** area. Her city is big, busy, and crowded.

3 Marcos lives in a **rural** area. His home is in the country. He lives on a quiet farm far from his neighbors.

Key Words

salvage

urban

rural

vacant

creative

reuse

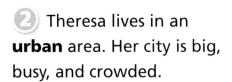

④ Workers tore down some old buildings. Now the lots are **vacant**.

⑤ The artist is very **creative**. She thought of a way to **reuse** things she found at the recycling center.

Practice

Use each key word in a sentence.

Make Connections

Reduce, reuse, and recycle: these are three ways to protect Earth's resources. What are some things that you recycle or reuse? Share your ideas with a partner.

Academic Words

construction
the process of building something

despite
although something is true

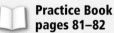
**Practice Book
pages 81–82**

INFORMATIONAL TEXT

Social Studies

The Big Question

What problems do we solve by using old things in new ways?

Reading Strategy

Identify Cause and Effect

- Identify what caused some buildings to be saved.

- Identify some effects of saving the old buildings.

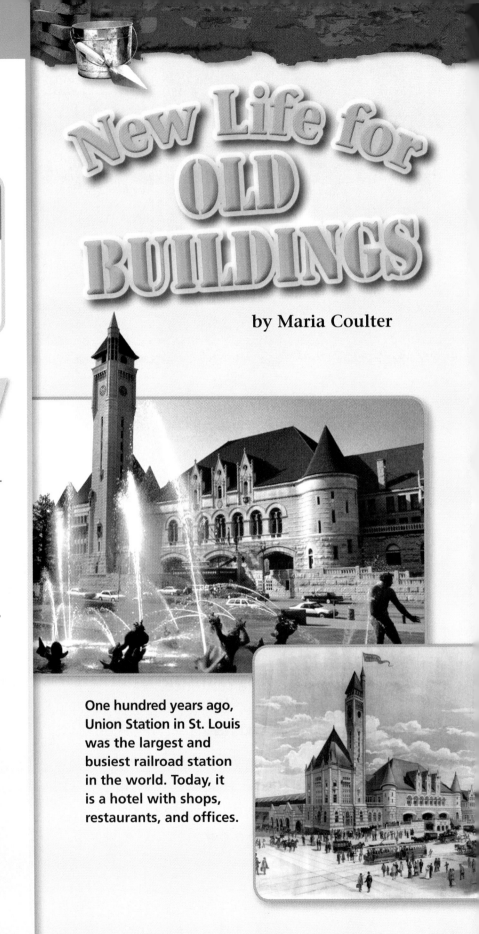

New Life for OLD BUILDINGS

by Maria Coulter

One hundred years ago, Union Station in St. Louis was the largest and busiest railroad station in the world. Today, it is a hotel with shops, restaurants, and offices.

You might be surprised to know that buildings are like people in some ways. Like people, they have a story to tell. Like each person, each building has a past.

Now, communities are trying to preserve their old buildings. Factories, train stations, churches, and schools are getting new lives!

Have you ever visited an old building and wondered about its history? Did you try to picture who lived or worked there? Imagine visiting an art gallery that was once a jail. Now it holds art instead of prisoners.

---

communities towns or areas where groups of people live

preserve save

jail place where criminals are kept when they are punished

Check Up ➤ **What was the effect of saving Union Station in St. Louis?**

A Missouri artist bought this old police station. Now it is the Mad Art Gallery.

One Iowa family lived in the Brucemore Mansion. Now it is a **cultural center** for everyone.

Not long ago, people tore down old buildings. Usually, they **replaced** old buildings with new ones. Sometimes they just left empty lots. When these buildings came down, people lost important **links** to the past.

People have learned that they can use an old building for a new purpose. They are finding creative ways to reuse buildings. Mansions have become museums. Schools have become apartment buildings. Railroad stations have become shopping centers.

---

cultural center   place for art, music, talks, and meetings

replaced   put something new in the place of something broken or old

links   things that connect something with something else

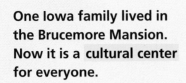

People in Littleton, Colorado, built this train station in 1888. It was empty for years. Then it became the Depot Art Center and Gallery.

In Delray, Florida, people turned an elementary school into the Cornell Museum of Art and History.

Abraham Lincoln once worked in this Springfield, Illinois, building. It was built in 1839. The Old State Capitol is now a museum.

There are good reasons to salvage old buildings.

Many old buildings were made with stone and brick. They are often strong and beautiful. Architects designed them to last a long time.

Abraham Lincoln was the 16th president of the United States.

Vacant buildings are a problem in urban and rural areas. Rescuing these buildings is a popular solution.

---

architects   people who design buildings

rescuing   saving

solution   way to solve a problem

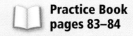
Practice Book
pages 83–84

Reading Strategy

Identify Cause and Effect

As you read this selection, you looked for causes and effects.

- What examples of causes and effects did you identify?

- Did looking for causes and effects help you to understand the selection? How?

Think It Over

1 What is this selection about?

2 How can an old building be a link to the past?

3 Name two good reasons to save old buildings.

Phonics & Fluency

Phonics

Digraph: *ow*

Sometimes the letters *ow* make one sound.

Words with digraph *ow*	
grow	cow
own	down
yellow	flower

What two vowel sounds do the letters *ow* have?

Rule Box

The letters *ow* can have the long *o* sound you hear in **low** or the vowel sound you hear in **how**. Some words, such as **bow**, have two meanings and can be pronounced either way.

Practice

Read the sentences with a partner. Look for words with *ow*.

- How can you help celebrate Preservation Month?
- Get to know the history of your hometown.
- Collect "then and now" photos to show at the library.

1. List the words in which **ow** has the long **o** sound heard in **low**.

2. List the words in which **ow** has the vowel sound heard in **how**.

Practice Book

page 85

174

Fluency

Look Ahead

Sometimes readers look for hard words before they read. Then they try to figure them out.

Practice

| Pick one passage. | Find any hard words. | Practice saying those words. | Read the passage aloud. |

1 Today, people use some old buildings in new ways. Railroad stations can become shopping centers. By reusing old buildings, people save links to their past.

2 Sometimes they just left empty lots. When these places came down, we lost important links to the past. People have learned that they can use an old building for a new purpose. They are finding creative ways to reuse buildings.

3 Schools have become apartment buildings. Railroad stations have become shopping centers. There are good reasons to salvage old buildings. Many old buildings were made with stone and brick. They are often strong and beautiful. Architects designed them to last a long time. Vacant buildings are a problem in urban and rural areas. Rescuing these buildings is a popular solution.

Comprehension

Cause and Effect

Finding cause and effect relationships can help you to understand what you read.

- The **cause** is why something happens.
- The **effect** is the thing that happens. It is the result of the cause.

To find an effect in a story, ask yourself: "What happened?" To find the cause, ask yourself: "Why did this thing happen?"

Practice

Read the sentences below with a partner.

- Make a chart with two columns. Write "Cause" in one column. Write "Effect" in the other column.
- List each cause and each effect in the correct column.

1. Katie heated the tea kettle. The water started to boil.

2. Stan studies every day. Stan does well on quizzes.

3. The baseball broke the window. Tom hit the baseball.

4. Plants grew in the field. The farmer planted seeds.

 Practice Book page 86

Use a Cause and Effect Chart

You can use a Cause and Effect Chart to help you understand cause and effect relationships in a story.

Practice

Copy and complete this Cause and Effect Chart for *New Life for Old Buildings*. Then compare your completed chart with a partner's.

Cause		Effect
Communities are trying to preserve their old buildings.	→	
	→	A jail now holds art instead of prisoners.
Many old buildings were made with stone and brick. They are often strong and beautiful.	→	

Extension

Are people using old buildings in your neighborhood in new ways? Are there any buildings you would like to save? Tell your class about them.

Grammar & Writing

Adverbs

Adverbs are words that tell about verbs. They add information by telling how something happens.

The words in red are adverbs.

Communities work **hard** to preserve their past.

The mayor acted **quickly** to save the vacant building.

Many adverbs end in -*ly*, like ***quickly***.

Practice

Read the sentences with a partner. List the adverbs. Look for words that tell how something happens.

1. Long ago, workers busily made furniture in that factory.

2. People in town looked sadly at the empty building.

3. They decided to work together.

4. The architect happily created a plan.

5. The mayor gladly supported the project.

6. She proudly announced the opening of the museum.

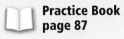

Practice Book page 87

Write a Cause and Effect Essay

There are many ways to write about cause and effect. Latisha wrote about a sport she enjoys.

> I love windsurfing. It started when I saw my Uncle Jed happily windsurfing at the lake. He stood on a sailboard. It looked like a surfboard, but it had a sail. When wind filled the sail, Jed sailed smoothly over the water.
>
> I was amazed. I wanted to windsurf, too! Uncle Jed taught me how. He let me use his board. At first, I fell all the time. Splash! It's hard to keep the board steady. I started windsurfing because I saw Uncle Jed. Now I have my own sailboard. I windsurf every day because it is so much fun!

SPELLING TIP

Sometimes the /f/ sound is not spelled with the letter *f*. In the words **photograph**, **microphone**, and **pharmacy**, the letters *ph* spell /f/.

Practice Book page 88

Practice

Write your own cause and effect essay. You might write about why you love a sport or hobby. You might write about why you dislike a dog in your neighborhood. Use a Cause and Effect Chart to help you organize your thinking.

Writing Checklist

✓ Did your introduction let your reader know that you would tell the cause of something or explain its effect?

✓ Did you use adverbs to make the action lively?

✓ Can a partner understand your description?

Running for Office

Key Words

government

candidates

campaign

law

politics

office

Vocabulary

Running for Office tells about the people we vote for.

Words in Context

1 In the United States, people choose **government** leaders in elections. For example, voters choose the president once every four years.

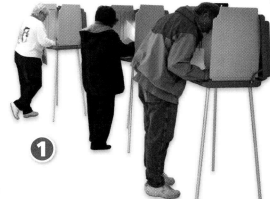

2 **Candidates** are people who want a government job. They **campaign**, or try to win, by meeting with voters.

3 Government leaders can make a **law** to solve or prevent problems. **Politics** means everything to do with government, leaders and political parties.

4 People who compete for any government **office** must understand the needs of their community.

Practice

Use each key word in a sentence.

Make Connections

What do you know about the U.S. government? Who is the president of the United States? Do you know the name of the governor of your state?

Academic Words

commit

say that you will definitely do something

ensure

make sure

Practice Book
pages 89–90

The **Big** Question

What kinds of problems do candidates want to solve?

Reading Strategy

Set a Purpose for Reading

Before you read, think about your purpose for reading. Are you reading

- to be entertained?
- to learn more about a topic?
- to form an opinion?

As you read this selection, keep your purpose in mind.

Running for Office

by Thomas P. Lee

Would you like to be president one day? Well, before you can be president you have to know the law. You also must understand government policy. Then you have to work hard to win an election .

President Clinton greets voters.

---

election   a time when people vote

Candidates must ask people to vote for them.

Politicians are people who like to help others. When they see a problem, they want to fix it. Mayors are politicians. The president is a politican, too. They each have a job in the government. A mayor works for the city or town. The president works for the country. Both use their government job to make life better for everyone.

Before a person can be a politician, they have to get the job. They get the job when they are elected. When they campaign, or run for office, they are asking people to vote for them.

---

politicians   people who run for or hold a government office

elected   chosen or decided by voting

Check Up ▸ How are a mayor and the president different?

Campaign signs appear during elections.

Every candidate has a message. "I will make our community better," they promise. They use posters and buttons that say, "Vote for me!"

A life in politics isn't always easy. Candidates need everyone's vote. So they must meet the voters. They greet shoppers at stores and say hello to people on the street. They put advertisements in newspapers. Sometimes, they debate the other candidates. Each person thinks he or she can do the best job. But they have to share their good ideas with voters.

---

greet say hello to someone

debate discuss a subject with people who have different opinions

Voters sometimes wear campaign buttons.

184

John F. Kennedy and Richard Nixon debated in 1960.

Candidates promise to do what the people want. Then on Election Day, the people vote. Everyone waits to see who wins. It is an exciting time. The winner is happy. He or she can now help their community.

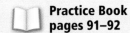
Practice Book pages 91–92

Reading Strategy

Set a Purpose for Reading

As you read this selection, you were asked to set a purpose for reading.

- What was your purpose for reading this selection?
- Did setting a purpose before reading help you understand this article? How?

Think It Over

1 What is this selection about?

2 Why do you think people run for office?

3 Why do candidates want to win elections?

185

Politicians

Support ▶
Politicians ask people to help them and vote for them.

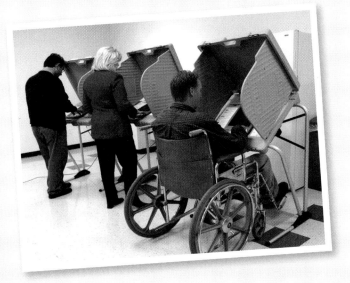

▲ **First president**
George Washington is called the Father of Our Country.

Election day ▶
Voters make their choices in a voting booth.

◄ Debate
Candidates debate ideas that are important to voters.

Candidates ►
All these people want the same government job.

▲ Campaign buttons
Voters wear buttons to show which candidates they like.

Activity to Do!

These two pages use pictures and words to tell about politicians.

- Imagine you were a politician. What would you say to voters?

- Design a campaign poster for yourself or a candidate you like.

187

Phonics & Fluency

Phonics

Soft and Hard c

Notice the difference between soft c and hard c.

Soft c	Hard c
celebrate	campaign
decide	discuss
policy	corner

When does c have the same sound as the s in **sun**?

When does c have the same sound as the k in **kite**?

Rule Box

The letter c usually has the soft sound when it is followed by e, i, or y. Otherwise, c usually has the hard sound.

Practice

Use a word from the chart to match each clue.

1. It's what you do when you choose something. (soft c)

2. It's what candidates do to win an election. (hard c)

3. It's the point where two walls meet. (hard c)

4. It's what candidates do when they win an election. (soft c)

5. It's another word for talk. (hard c)

Practice Book

page 93

Fluency

Read for Speed and Accuracy

You should read quickly. But never read so quickly that you lose your understanding.

Practice

| Read for one minute. | | Count the words you read. | | Study any hard words. | | Read and count again. |

Every candidate has a message. "I will make our	9
community better," they promise. They use posters and	17
buttons that say, "Vote for me!"	23
A life in politics isn't always easy. Candidates need	32
everyone's vote. So they must meet the voters. They greet	42
shoppers at stores and say hello to people on the street.	53
They put advertisements in newspapers. Sometimes, they	60
debate the other candidates. Each person thinks he or	69
she can do the best job. But they have to share their good	82
ideas with voters.	85
Candidates promise to do what the people want. Then	94
on Election Day, the people vote.	100

Comprehension

Retell

Retell the selection to a partner.

 Ask your partner to respond to the Big Question for this reading.

The 5 W Questions

Before you read, think about your purpose for reading. Do you want to learn something? Ask yourself the 5 W quesions:

- Who?
- What?
- Where?
- When?
- Why?

Practice

With a partner, read *Running for Office* again. Review the photo captions. Look for answers to the following questions.

1. Who are candidates?

2. What do they do?

3. Where do they run for office?

4. When do people vote?

5. Why do candidates run for office?

Use a 5 W Chart

A 5 W Chart helps you find the information you need in a selection. Think about each *W* question. Then look for the answers as you read.

Practice

Copy the chart. Use the 5 W questions to show what you learned from reading *Running for Office*.

Who?	
What?	
Where?	
When?	
Why?	

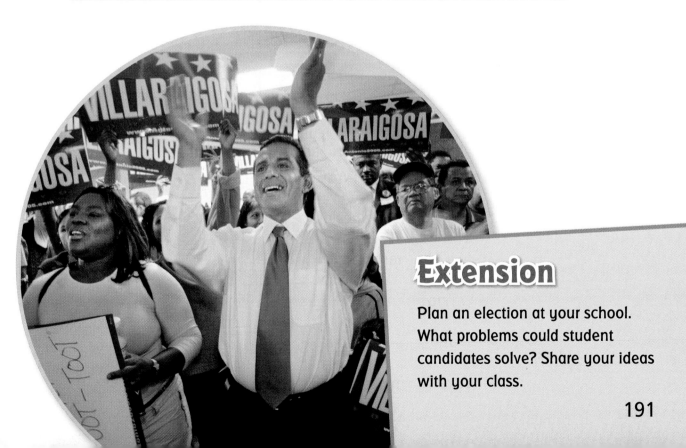

Extension

Plan an election at your school. What problems could student candidates solve? Share your ideas with your class.

Grammar & Writing

Four Kinds of Sentences

A **declarative sentence** states, or tells, something.

This declarative sentence tells what candidates do.

> Candidates try to win an election.

This chart shows four kinds of sentences.

Kind of Sentence	Example
A **declarative** sentence tells something.	I am running for class president.
An **interrogative** sentence asks something.	Do you think she will win?
An **imperative** sentence gives a command.	Listen to my speech.
An **exclamatory** sentence expresses strong feeling.	You were great!

Practice

Work with a partner. Tell whether each sentence is interrogative, declarative, imperative, or exclamatory.

1. The election takes place tomorrow.

2. Are you nervous?

3. I'm not nervous, but I am excited.

4. I can't wait to vote!

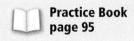
Practice Book page 95

5. Vote for my candidate.

Write from Different Points of View

You can use a chart to help you compare and contrast two people's points of view.

I Like Uniforms (Daisy)	I Don't Like Uniforms (Anita)
Yes, I do like uniforms.	I do not like uniforms.
I like wearing the same thing every day.	I want to wear something different every day.
I don't like shopping for clothes.	I love shopping for clothes.

Daisy and Anita wrote their points of view. Can you tell who wrote which paragraph?

> Do I like school uniforms? Yes, I do! I don't like shopping for clothes. Also, I like wearing the same thing every day. I don't have to think about choosing what to wear.

> I hate uniforms! I like wearing pretty clothes. It's fun to wear something different every day. I love shopping for clothes. Please, don't make us wear uniforms.

SPELLING TIP

The letter *g* stands for two sounds: /g/ and /j/. Many words beginning with *g* have the /g/ sound: *good, gave*. If the vowels *i* or *e* follow *g*, the sound may be /j/: *giant, gentle*.

Practice Book page 96

Practice

Think of a topic that you and a friend do not agree on. Write one paragraph for each point of view. Paraphrase the two points of view for your class.

Writing Checklist

✓ Did you show two points of view?

✓ Did you use different kinds of sentences?

✓ Did your class understand your paraphrasing?

PROBLEMS
Stop London Eye

Vocabulary

The next selection is a newspaper article. It tells about a time when workers had to repair a famous ferris wheel.

Words in Context

Key Words

opportunity

research

fair

attraction

suggested

persuade

1 Once a year, every student writes an essay about fire safety. The student who writes the best essay gets the **opportunity** to ride in a real fire truck.

2 The scientist went to the forest to do **research**. She is studying birds.

③ The county **fair** is a big outdoor party. I like the contests, rides, and music. My favorite **attraction** is the merry-go-round.

④ My friends **suggested** that I buy red shoes. My mother tried to **persuade** me to buy brown ones instead. She said they would look nicer.

Practice

Use each key word in a sentence.

Make Connections

Many scientists do research. They want to learn more about the world. If you were a scientist, what would you study?

Academic Words

convince

make someone believe something is true

---

enormous

very large

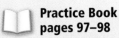

Practice Book pages 97–98

The Big Question

How do inventions help people solve problems?

Reading Strategy

Compare and Contrast

- Look at the pictures of the two ferris wheels.
- Think about the ways the ferris wheels are alike.
- Think about the ways they are different.

PROBLEMS
Stop London Eye

by Archie Hurbane

More than 3.5 million people ride the London Eye each year.

LONDON, ENGLAND, March 2 —The world's largest ferris wheel stood still yesterday. There was a problem with its motor. The London Eye would not spin around.

"This is bad news," said 9-year-old Martin Moore. "I want to ride the Eye. It's my birthday."

The Eye was opened on New Year's Eve, 1999. It is England's most popular visitor attraction. The Eye is 443 feet high. Every year, about 3.5 million people have the opportunity to ride it. But yesterday, people had to wait.

One person waiting was history teacher Hannah Demayo. She shared her research on ferris wheels. She explained that the first ferris wheel was invented more than 100 years ago.

The Eiffel Tower is in Paris, France.

"Paris built the Eiffel Tower for the 1889 World's Fair," said Ms. DeMayo. "It became a famous symbol of the city. Other cities wanted their own symbol."

motor   machine that gives the power to make something work

spin   turn around and around very quickly

invented   newly created

symbol   design or object that represents, or stands for, something else

Check Up ▸ **How are the boy and the teacher the same?**

The first ferris wheel was taller than most buildings in Chicago.

George Ferris invented the ferris wheel.

"The Eiffel Tower became the world's tallest structure. Then, four years after it was built, Chicago had the next World's Fair," continued Ms. DeMayo.

"Did Chicago build a tower, too?" asked Mr. Moore.

"No, but Chicago had a problem," said Ms. DeMayo. "It needed its own attraction."

She told everyone about George Ferris. "He suggested that the city build a huge wheel. He believed many people would want to ride it."

Mr. Ferris was right. His 140-foot wheel was a great success. And now there are ferris wheels in fairs everywhere.

structure   something that has been built

huge   very large

success   good result

Suddenly a worker spoke.

"Thank you for your patience," he said. "Can I persuade you to wait a little longer? We are almost ready."

Soon, the Eye was spinning again. The crowd was happy. And Mr. Moore got his birthday wish. He rode the Eye high into the London sky.

In 1893, people rode the first ferris wheel in Chicago.

---

patience ability to wait without getting angry

crowd large group of people

wish strong hope

Practice Book
pages 99–100

Reading Strategy

Compare and Contrast

As you read this selection, you were asked to compare and contrast.

- What did you compare? What did you contrast?

- Did comparing and contrasting help you understand the news article? How?

Think It Over

1 What is this news article about?

2 Why did George Ferris invent the ferris wheel?

3 Why do you think people like riding on ferris wheels?

Word Analysis & Fluency

Word Analysis

Thesaurus

A **dictionary** tells the meaning of a word. A **thesaurus** lists synonyms for a word, or words with similar meanings.

Read this sentence.

> Historian Hannah Demayo told the **crowd** about her research.

If you wanted to know the meaning of the word *crowd,* you would look up the word in a dictionary. If you wanted to find a synonym for *crowd,* a thesaurus would help you choose the best word.

Practice

Work with a partner.
- Read the sentence and the thesaurus entry that follows.
- Choose the synonym that could go in that sentence.

> "This is **bad** news," said customer Martin Moore.

bad *adj.* **1.** terrible. **2.** wrong. **3.** harmful. **4.** sick.

Fluency

Read with Expression

When you read aloud, use your voice to show feelings.

Practice

| Read silently. | | Read aloud. | | Get comments. | | Read aloud again. |

"The Eiffel Tower became the world's tallest structure. Then, four years after it was built, Chicago had the next World's Fair," continued Ms. DeMayo.

"Did Chicago build a tower, too?" asked Mr. Moore.

"No, but Chicago had a problem," said Ms. DeMayo. "It needed its own attraction."

She told everyone about George Ferris. "He suggested that the city build a huge wheel. He believed many people would want to ride it."

Mr. Ferris was right. His 140-foot wheel was a great success. And now there are ferris wheels in fairs everywhere.

Comprehension

Compare and Contrast

To understand what you read, compare and contrast ideas.

- When you **compare**, you tell how two or more things are alike.
- When you **contrast**, you tell how two or more things are different.

Compare and contrast the items listed or shown in each exercise. Tell two ways they are alike. Then tell two ways they are different.

1. a fishbowl and a pool

2. a car and a bicycle

3.

Practice Book page 102

Use a T-Chart

You can use a T-Chart to compare and contrast events, characters, or objects in a story or a nonfiction selection.

Practice

Copy the T-Chart. Compare and contrast the two items.

1. Write about how the London Eye and the 1892 ferris wheel are the same. Use the pictures and the words in the selection to help you.

2. Then write about how they are different.

3. Compare your completed T-Chart with a partner's.

How They Are Alike	How They Are Different

Extension

Think about other amusement park rides. Compare and contrast two rides. You can write descriptions, draw them, or act them out. Show your class how they are alike and how they are different.

Grammar & Writing

Compound Words

Like many fairs, the 1892 World's Fair took place in an open space called a fairground.

The word *fairground* is a compound word — a word made up of two shorter words. One word is *fair*, which can mean an outdoor event with games, rides, and entertainment. The other word is *ground*, which can mean land used for a special purpose.

Practice

Find the compound word in each sentence.

1. I am meeting my cousin at the airport.

2. There are raindrops on the window.

3. Look at the newspaper article.

4. Tomorrow is Alberto's birthday.

5. We will give him a basketball as a present.

6. The chef found the recipe in her cookbook.

Practice Book page 103

Write a Newspaper Article

Tim's newspaper article answers the 5 W questions.

	Big Fish	**Meat and Potatoes**
Who	Chef Polly	Chef Tom
What	seafood restaurant. prettier, quieter	restaurant. serves burgers, more fun
Where	Fargo Mall	Main Street
When	opened last week	opened last week
Why	owner wanted a fancy restaurant	owner wanted a friendly restaurant

Fargo, ND, May 18 — Two new restaurants opened last week. Both have good food, but the restaurants are different.

Big Fish is in Fargo Mall. It is pretty and quiet. The seafood is delicious. Chef Polly wanted a fancy restaurant.

Meat and Potatoes is on Main Street. It is not pretty, and the music is loud. But the burgers are great. Meat and Potatoes is not as fancy as Big Fish, but it is more fun. Chef Tom wanted a friendly restaurant.

SPELLING TIP

How can you find a word in the dictionary if you don't know how to spell it? Say the word. What is the first sound? Write that letter. Then say the word again, listen to the next sound, and write it down. Soon, you will have enough letters to help you find the word.

Practice Book page 104

Practice

- Write a newspaper article that compares two restaurants.
- Use a 5 W Chart to organize your ideas.

Writing Checklist

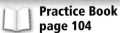

✓ Did your article tell about things that are alike and things that are different?

✓ Did you answer each of the 5 W questions?

✓ Can a partner understand your descriptions?

205

The Trouble with Kudzu

by Laura Sewell

Big, beautiful leaves and sweet-smelling purple flowers made kudzu popular.

This old truck is not going anywhere!

Do you know the story of Jack and the Beanstalk? Jack planted a magic bean. A vine grew from the bean. It grew and grew. Finally, the vine was so high and strong that Jack could climb up it and reach the clouds.

Well, kudzu doesn't come from a magic bean, but it is a member of the bean family. When people saw kudzu for the first time, they must have thought it was magic. Why? Because kudzu grows very fast — much faster than most other plants. In fact, it can grow up to 12 inches in only one day!

Kudzu is a native plant of China and Japan. That means it grew naturally in those countries. Kudzu was brought to the United States from Japan in 1876 as a gift. The United States was celebrating its first 100 years as a nation.

Americans first saw kudzu at the 1876 Centennial Exhibition in Philadelphia.

Soon, every gardener and farmer wanted to plant kudzu seeds. Gardeners grew kudzu because it looked pretty and smelled good. Farmers grew it to feed their animals.

At first, kudzu was a big success! But it did not stop growing. It blocked sunlight that other plants needed. It killed trees and whole forests. Nothing was safe!

Where have the trees gone? They are all covered with kudzu!

It takes only two or three years for kudzu to cover a house.

Now, people call kudzu a weed. It is a wild plant that grows where it is not wanted. People cut it down and dig up its roots. But getting rid of kudzu is not easy.

Over the years, people have learned to use every part of the kudzu plant. Cooks and artists use it to make jelly, paper, clothes, baskets, and chairs. This weed might be useful after all.

Artist Nancy Basket makes baskets with kudzu.

The Big Question

How do people solve problems?

Written	Oral	 Visual/Active
Skit	**Fable**	**Flowchart of Steps**
Choose one of the selections. Write a skit about the problem and how it was solved. Make sure the lesson is clear.	Many fables are about solving a problem. The way a character solves a problem leads to a lesson. Write a fable about someone who must solve a problem.	Think of a problem you read about and how it was solved. Identify the problem. Tell what steps were taken to solve it. Then explain the solution.
News Article	**Interview**	**Comic Strip**
Write a newspaper article about a problem in your community. Tell how people solved it. Answer the 5 W questions in your article.	Interview someone who has solved a problem. Find out what the problem was. Tell how the person solved it. Record your interview.	Create a comic strip about a problem and how it is solved. Use a problem you read about, or think of your own problem.
Building Proposal	**Speech**	**Matching Game**
Write a proposal telling how a building in your community could be put to a different use. Tell how this will solve a problem.	Deliver a speech that you would give if you were running for office. Describe a problem and how you would solve it.	Create two sets of cards. One set shows problems. The other shows their solutions. Mix the cards. Challenge players to match problem cards with solution cards.

✔ Learning Checklist

Phonics and Word Analysis

✓ Read words in which the diagraph *ow* stands for one vowel sound.

✓ Identify soft and hard c.

✓ Use a thesaurus.

Comprehension

✓ Identify causes and effects.

✓ Use a Cause and Effect Chart.

✓ Set purposes for reading using the 5 W questions.

✓ Use a Five W Chart.

✓ Look for comparisons and contrasts.

✓ Create a T-Chart.

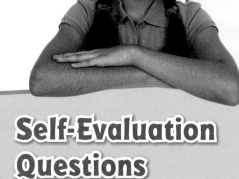

Grammar and Writing

✓ Identify adverbs.

✓ Recognize the four kinds of sentences.

✓ Recognize and use compound words.

✓ Write a cause and effect essay.

✓ Write from different points of view.

✓ Write a newspaper article.

Self-Evaluation Questions

• How does what you learned connect to other subjects in school?

• What questions do you still have?

• How does what you've learned relate to your community?

UNIT 5

Where We Live

You will learn about different homes around the world. All of the selections are informational. Each was written to tell you about houses.

READINGS

The Underground City

A House of Grass

Living in the Trees

? **The Big Question**
What is it like
to live in an
unusual home?

LISTENING AND SPEAKING

You will talk about where you live and where you would like to live.

Life at the Top of the World

WRITING

You will write a speech about something important to your school, home, or community.

Quick Write

Do any of these homes look familiar to you? Explain why.

What Do You Know about Where People Live?

Words to Know

1. Use these words to talk about the places people live.

 townhouse

 houseboat

 apartment

 retirement home

 mobile home

 single family home

---

2. Where do you live?

I live in _____ .

 a townhouse

 a retirement home

 a houseboat

 a mobile home

 an apartment

 a single family home

214

3. What can you do where you live?

In my _____ *, I can* _____ .

vacuum the carpet

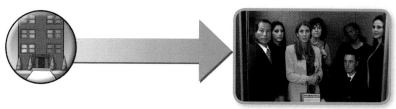

ride in the elevator

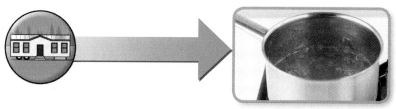

cook a meal

jump in the ocean

4. What are some other places people live?

igloo

log cabin

treehouse

teepee

Your Stories about Where We Live

China

New Guinea

Xiaohong

I live in China. Many families here live on boats. My family has a houseboat. We have a fishing business. My father and my brother take the boat into the ocean. They catch fish. Then they return to the harbor. I eat the fish they bring home.

Rabbie

I live in Papua New Guinea. In my country, some native people live in treehouses. Some families live in trees that are 80 feet high! I live in a house on the ground. But I hope to live in a treehouse one day.

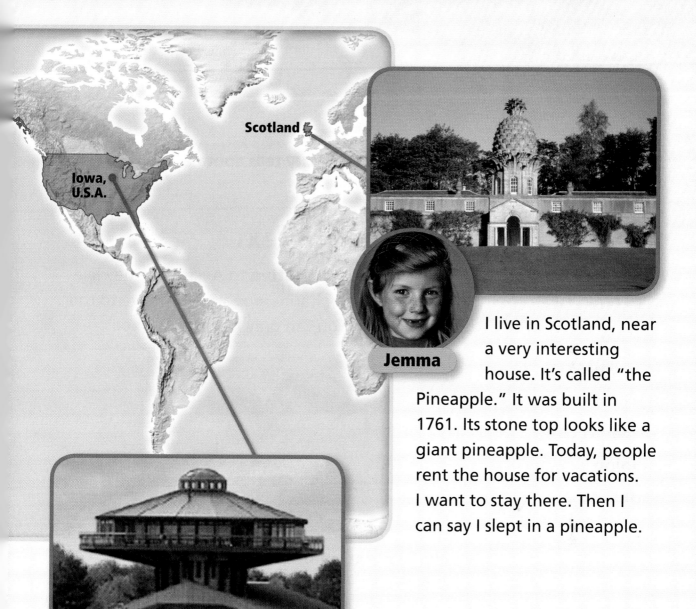

Jemma

I live in Scotland, near a very interesting house. It's called "the Pineapple." It was built in 1761. Its stone top looks like a giant pineapple. Today, people rent the house for vacations. I want to stay there. Then I can say I slept in a pineapple.

Carlito

I live in Iowa. People come from far away to see the "spaceship house" in my town. The house has a round room that is 57 feet long. It looks just like a spaceship. I think it would be fun to live in this house!

What about you?

1 What is your home like?

2 How are these students' stories similar to yours?

3 Do you have other stories about unusual homes? Tell your story!

217

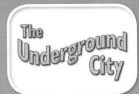

The
Underground
City

Vocabulary

The Underground City tells about a town where people live in caves.

Words in Context

1 Kangaroos are **native** to Australia. They live in the wild there. Kangaroos are not native to the United States. You can only find them in zoos.

2 The United States is a big country. Some parts have **extreme**, or great, heat. Others have extreme cold.

Key Words

native

extreme

architecture

underground

mining

efficient

3 Styles of **architecture** change with time. Look at these two museums. Which one is an older style? How do you know?

4 Coal and gold are found **underground.** They are deep under Earth's surface. We get them by **mining**. Workers dig down to where the coal or gold is. Then they bring it up to the surface.

5 Being **efficient** means working quickly and well. When you are efficient, you do not waste time.

Practice

Use each key word in a sentence.

Make Connections

Have you ever been in a cave? Was it warm or cold? Was it damp or dry? Why do you think some people like living in caves?

Academic Words

survive

stay alive

unique

one of a kind

 Practice Book pages 107–108

FUNCTIONAL WRITING

Magazine Article

The **Big** Question

Why is it important that people and animals adapt their homes to their environment?

Reading Strategy

Identify
Fact and Opinion

- A fact is something that is real or true. You can prove something is a fact.

- An opinion is what someone thinks about something. You cannot prove an opinion is true or false.

- As you read, look for facts and opinions.

The Underground City

by Claudio Ponti

Have you ever seen a house that is under the ground? Come visit a town called Coober Pedy!

The town of Coober Pedy is in southern Australia.

A man plays a game in his underground home.

About 3,500 people live in Coober Pedy, Australia. From the street, you might see only dirt and some trees. But under the ground, there are homes! More than half of the people in the town live in underground houses. These are regular houses. They look a lot like yours!

The summer heat in Coober Pedy is extreme. But the underground homes are efficient. They stay cool during the hot months. That means people don't spend money on air conditioning. In the winter, the homes stay warm. That means people pay less for heat.

The underground houses look just like regular homes.

Check Up Name two facts about Coober Pedy.

---

air conditioning   system that makes air cooler and drier

Opals are beautiful gems that are used for jewelry.

Opals are native to Coober Pedy. Most of the people who live there work in the opal business. They dig up opals from under the ground. Then they sell the opals to people all over the world.

The first opal was found in Coober Pedy in 1915. Soon, mining became popular there. The miners noticed how cool the air was inside the mines. These men had slept in trenches in World War I. They knew that living under the ground was cooler than living in the desert heat. That's how the underground homes began.

Soldiers in World War I slept in trenches below the ground.

business   buying or selling of goods and services

trenches   long, narrow holes dug into the ground

desert   large area of land that is very dry and usually very hot

In Coober Pedy, people dig out dirt and leave it in big piles.

Hello Max,

I am in Coober Pedy. It is a special town in Australia. Many visitors come to see the underground architecture. The people who live in Coober Pedy work hard in the heat all day. They spend many hours drilling for opals. At the end of the day, they go to their nice, cool homes. They live in underground caves!

I'll see you soon!

Meghan

I saw workers use large machines to dig opals out of the ground.

visitors   people who come to see a place or a person

Practice Book
pages 109–110

Reading Strategy

Identify Fact and Opinion

- What is one fact about Coober Pedy?
- What is your opinion of Coober Pedy?
- Did looking for facts and opinions help you understand the selection? How?

Think It Over

1 What country is Coober Pedy in?

2 How many of the homes in Coober Pedy are underground?

3 Why do you think most people in Coober Pedy work in the opal business?

223

Caves

▲ Stalactites

Stalactites are minerals. They hang from the tops of many caves.

▲ Cave cities

In the past, some people carved cities in the hills.

Bats ▶

Caves are homes for bats and other animals.

◀ Cave art

People made cave paintings thousands of years ago.

◀ Hibernate
Bears hibernate, or sleep during the winter, in caves.

Spelunker ▶
Spelunkers are people who like to explore caves.

▲ Ice cave
This cave is found in mountain ice.

Activity to Do!

These two pages use pictures and words to tell about caves.

- Pick any cave that interests you.
- Research that cave.
- Create two pages to tell about that cave. Use pictures and captions.

225

Word Analysis & Fluency

Word Analysis

Homophones

How are the words in red alike?
How are they different?

> Do the stores in Coober Pedy **sell** opals?
>
> Is there an underground jail **cell** in town?

The words *sell* and *cell* sound the same, but they have different spellings and different meanings. They are **homophones**.

- In the first sentence, *sell* means "to give for money."
- In the second sentence, *cell* means "a small room in a jail."

Practice

Write each sentence. Use the correct homophone.

1. I _____ like to visit Coober Pedy. (wood, would)
   CLUE: Which word relates to the word *will*?

2. I want to meet the people who live _____. (their, there)
   CLUE: Which word means "in that place"?

3. We will _____ the miners at work. (sea, see)
   CLUE: Which word means "look at"?

4. She might _____ an opal. (buy, by)
   CLUE: Which word is the opposite of *sell*?

Fluency

Look Ahead

Sometimes readers look for hard words before they read.
They then try to figure them out.

Practice

| Pick one passage. | Find any hard words. | Practice saying those words. | Read the passage aloud. |

1. Coober Pedy, Australia, is a special town. Many people live in underground homes. Summer is very hot there. People built homes under the ground to stay cool. Today, many people come to visit the underground homes.

2. Opals are native to Coober Pedy. Most of the people who live there work in the opal business. They dig up opals from under the ground. Then they sell the opals to people all over the world.

3. The first opal was found in Coober Pedy in 1915. Soon, mining became popular there. The miners noticed how cool the air was inside the mines. These men had slept in trenches in World War I. They knew that living under the ground was cooler than living in the desert heat. That's how the underground homes began.

Comprehension

Fact and Opinion

A **fact** is something that can be proved. An **opinion** is what someone thinks. Words such as *great*, *amazing*, and *bad* are clues that you are reading opinions.

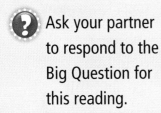

Practice

Tell whether each sentence states a fact or gives an opinion. If it is a fact, tell where you can find the proof.

1. The town of Coober Pedy is in Australia.

2. It must be hard to live underground.

3. About 3,500 people live in Coober Pedy.

4. People who live underground are probably very friendly.

5. Underground homes are cool in summer and warm in winter.

Practice Book

page 112

228

Use a Fact and Opinion Chart

A Fact and Opinion Chart helps you tell facts from opinions. First, list each fact or opinion in the correct column. Then, tell why you decided it was a fact or an opinion.

Practice

Sort the list of facts and opinions from the previous page. Explain your choice in the third column. Then answer the questions below.

Fact	Opinion	Why?
The town of Coober Pedy is in Australia.		You can prove it by looking on a map of Australia.
	It must be hard to live underground.	The word **hard** is a clue that this is an opinion.

1. Which sentence would you add to the Fact column?
   a. Opals are beautiful gems.
   b. The first opal was found in Coober Pedy in 1915.
   c. People who live underground are friendly.
   d. Coober Pedy is a special town.

2. How could you prove the fact that you chose?
   a. Ask a friend.
   b. Look it up in an encyclopedia.
   c. Read about it in a newspaper.
   d. Buy an opal.

3. Add another fact you learned from the selection. Tell how you can prove it is a fact.

Extension

How is living underground different from where you live? Would you like to live underground? Make a drawing that shows why or why not. Share your drawing with your class.

Grammar & Writing

Commas in Place Names and Dates

Commas are used in dates, numbers, and place names.

> About 3,500 people live in Coober Pedy, Australia.

Notice that the author used a comma between the name of the town and the name of the country. This chart shows more rules for using commas.

Rule	Example
Use a comma between the name of a city and its country.	Have you been to Paris, France?
Use a comma between the name of a city and its state.	We will visit Los Angeles, California.
Use a comma between the day and year.	My sister was born on March 21, 2003.

Practice

Write each sentence correctly.

1. My uncle sent us a postcard from Lima Peru.

2. He was born there on November 16 1964.

3. Today he lives in Baltimore Maryland.

4. My aunt moved to England on June 18 2007.

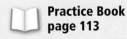
Practice Book page 113

Write a Persuasive Brochure

In a persuasive brochure, you try to convince someone to do something. Lilia wants to persuade people to come to the opening party for a sports center. Notice the kinds of information she gives.

Come to the opening of the new Morris Park Sports Center! The pool and gym will be open to everyone. Coach Johnson will judge a swimming contest. The town choir will sing their favorite songs. There will be games and prizes. Visit your new sports center. You might win a new tennis racket. You'll be glad you came!

Saturday, June 2, 2010
Morris Park Sports Center
2005 Morris Avenue
Storyville, NY 12783

SPELLING TIP

When the letter *c* makes the *s* sound, *e, i,* or *y* always follows the *c*.

cell, circus, certain, fancy

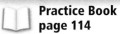 **Practice Book page 114**

Practice

Imagine that you are opening a new summer camp. Write a brochure, magazine ad, or poster to tell about it. Make the camp sound like fun! Be sure to include all the necessary information.

Writing Checklist

✓ Did you tell what the place is and what people do there?

✓ Did you include reasons why people will want to come?

✓ Can a partner understand all the information?

A House of Grass

Vocabulary

In *A House of Grass*, two cousins communicate through letters. One girl lives on the prairie. The other lives in a city.

Words in Context

Key Words

prairie

sod

climate

harsh

record

1 In summer, the **prairie** is full of flowers and tall grasses.

2 Some people scatter grass seed and wait for the grass to grow. Others buy rolls of **sod** and have lawns quickly.

232

3 The **climate** in this desert is **harsh**. It is always very dry. During the day, the desert gets very hot. At night, it gets very cold.

4 Our coach keeps a **record** of how many times we hit the ball.

Practice

Use each key word in a sentence.

Make Connections

Long ago, friends wrote letters to each other. How do friends communicate today? Which way do you like best? Why?

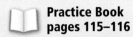
Practice Book
pages 115–116

FUNCTIONAL WRITING

Letters

The Big Question

In this selection, a young girl moves to a new home. Why would she write letters to her cousin back home?

Reading Strategy

Identify Author's Purpose

Before you read, think about the author's purpose for writing. Is the author writing

- to entertain?
- to tell about something?
- to persuade you to do or think something?

As you read, think about why Sarah and Molly wrote their letters.

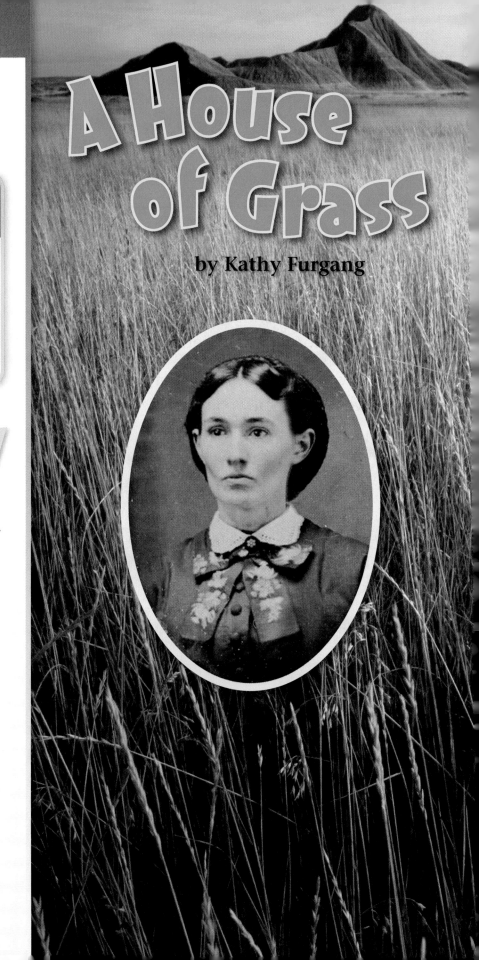

A House of Grass

by Kathy Furgang

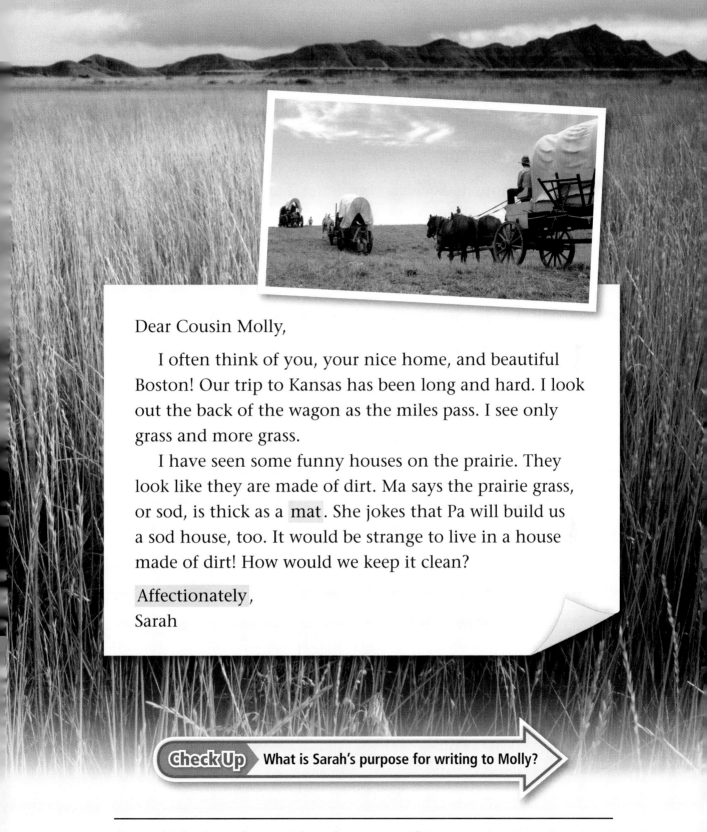

Dear Cousin Molly,

I often think of you, your nice home, and beautiful Boston! Our trip to Kansas has been long and hard. I look out the back of the wagon as the miles pass. I see only grass and more grass.

I have seen some funny houses on the prairie. They look like they are made of dirt. Ma says the prairie grass, or sod, is thick as a mat. She jokes that Pa will build us a sod house, too. It would be strange to live in a house made of dirt! How would we keep it clean?

Affectionately,
Sarah

CheckUp What is Sarah's purpose for writing to Molly?

mat   thick piece of material used to cover a floor

affectionately   gently showing love or caring

Dear Cousin Sarah,

I was happy to receive your letter. I am sure you now have a nice new home. Please tell me it is not made of dirt! Mother said sod houses are hard to live in. They are tiny, their roofs leak, and the dirt walls are filled with bugs!

Will you ever return to Boston? The prairie must be a difficult place to live. Life is easier here.

I hope you keep a diary. If you keep a record of your adventures, one day your children can learn about your new life.

Love,
Molly

---

receive   get from someone

difficult   not easy

diary   book in which you write things that happen each day

Dear Molly,

I have funny news! We live in a sod house! It is dark and damp. But do not worry. It will protect us from the climate. It is an excellent shelter!

There are few trees on the prairie. The land looks like a sea of grass.

People here have little money. But they are clever. Many can't buy wood, stone, or bricks. That is why people build with sod. They cut the sod into pieces. Then they stack the pieces like bricks to make things.

That is how Pa made our new house!

Love,
Sarah

CheckUp What does Molly tell Sarah about her prairie home?

---

damp moist or a little bit wet

clever creative and quick to learn

stack form a neat pile of things, one on top of the other

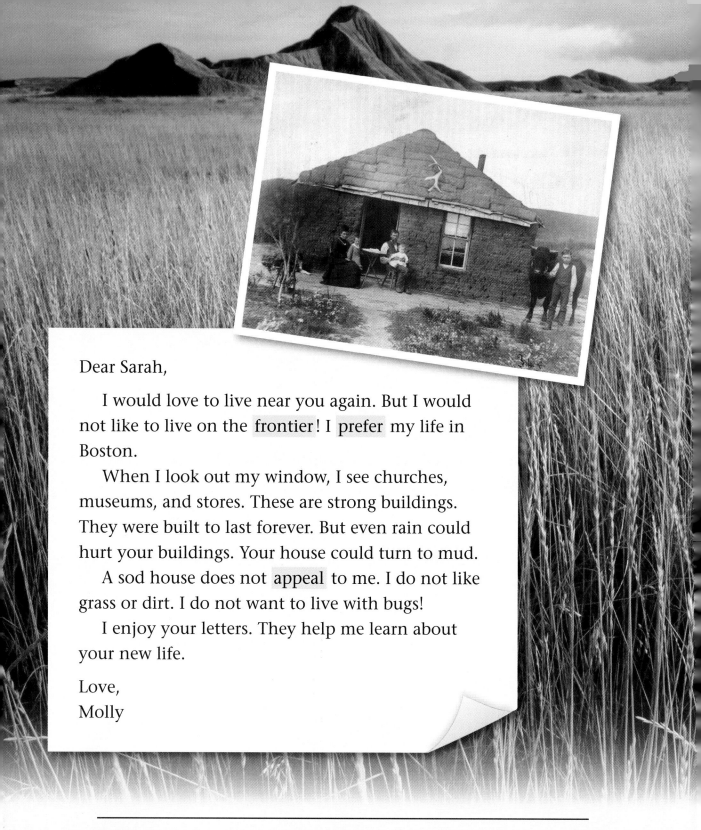

Dear Sarah,

I would love to live near you again. But I would not like to live on the frontier! I prefer my life in Boston.

When I look out my window, I see churches, museums, and stores. These are strong buildings. They were built to last forever. But even rain could hurt your buildings. Your house could turn to mud.

A sod house does not appeal to me. I do not like grass or dirt. I do not want to live with bugs!

I enjoy your letters. They help me learn about your new life.

Love,
Molly

---

frontier   area beyond places people know well

prefer   like better

appeal   seem interesting or fun

Dear Molly,

Do not worry about me and my little sod house. I agree that sometimes the climate is harsh. But our house is cool in summer and warm in winter.

I love my new life on the prairie. I know that someday more people will move to the frontier. We will build towns and cities. Then we will have all the comforts of Boston!

Your loving cousin,
Sarah

comforts   things that make life nicer

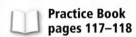

**Practice Book
pages 117–118**

Reading Strategy

Identify Author's Purpose

- Molly and Sarah had different reasons for writing their letters. What were they?

- Did thinking about the author's purpose help you to understand the selection? How?

Think It Over

1 Where does Sarah's family come from?

2 Why do people on the prairie use sod to build their houses?

3 Would you like to live in Sarah's house? Why or why not?

4 Why do people enjoy reading letters?

239

Phonics & Fluency

Phonics

Y as a Vowel

Sometimes the letter *y* acts as a vowel.

Y as a Vowel	
Long *i*	**Long *e***
by	city
dry	dirty
my	worry

Each word in the chart has the letter *y* at the end. Each word also has a consonant before the *y*.

When does the letter *y* have the long *i* sound? When does the letter *y* have the long *e* sound?

Rule Box

• The letter *y* usually has the long /i/ sound when it comes after a consonant at the end of a one-syllable word.

• The letter *y* usually has the long /e/ sound when it comes after a consonant at the end of a word with more than one syllable.

Practice

Read the sentences with a partner. Take turns.

• Molly lives in the city of Boston.
• My new home is in Kansas.
• It was not easy to move away.
• We have many stories to share.

1. List the words in which *y* has the long /i/ sound.
2. List the words in which *y* has the long /e/ sound.

Practice Book

page 119

240

Fluency

Read with Expression

When you read aloud, use your voice to show feelings.

Practice

| Read silently. | → | Read aloud. | → | Get comments. | → | Read aloud again. |

Dear Molly,

I have funny news! We live in a sod house! It is dark and damp. But do not worry. It will protect us from the climate. It is an excellent shelter!

There are few trees on the prairie. The land looks like a sea of grass.

People here have little money. But they are clever. Many can't buy wood, stone, or bricks. That is why people build with sod. They cut the sod into pieces. Then they stack the pieces like bricks to make things.

That is how Pa made our new house!

Love,
Sarah

Comprehension

Author's Purpose

Authors have purposes for writing. An author writes to entertain, persuade, or inform. Knowing the author's purpose will help you understand what you read.

Summarize

Summarize the selection for a partner.

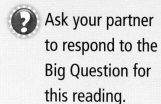 Ask your partner to respond to the Big Question for this reading.

Practice

Read the sentences. Tell if the author's purpose is to entertain, persuade, or inform. Explain your answers.

1. Sod houses are made of dirt. Today's houses are made of brick or wood.

2. You will love our sod house. When it rains, the roof leaks. Then mud falls on your head!

3. Sod houses and today's houses protect you from cold weather.

4. Sod houses are the best houses. They are cool in the summer and warm in the winter. You must build a sod house.

📖 **Practice Book page 120**

Use a Compare and Contrast Chart

A Compare and Contrast Chart can help you compare and contrast the information you read with what you already know.

- When you **compare**, you tell how two or more things are alike.
- When you **contrast**, you tell how they are different.

Practice

Copy and complete this chart. Use the questions below to help you.

1. What other information from the selection can you put in the Alike box?

2. What other information from the selection can you put in the Different box?

3. What information from your own experience can you put in the Alike box?

4. What information from your own experience can you put in the Different box?

Sod Houses
and
Today's Houses

Alike

protect from
bad weather

Different

Sod: dirt

Today: brick
or wood

Extension

Write a letter to Molly or Sarah. Tell about where you live. Include a drawing that shows some of your ideas. Share your drawing with your class.

Grammar & Writing

Commas in a Series

Writers use commas to separate three or more items in a series.

You can see museums and stores in Boston.

You can see churches, museums, and stores in Boston.

- In the first sentence, a comma is not needed to separate two items.

- In the second sentence, commas separate the three items in the series. A comma comes before the word *and*. There is no comma after the last item.

Practice

Write each sentence correctly. Use commas to separate items in a series.

1. Sarah her mother and her father traveled to Kansas.

2. Their sod house protected them from wind rain and snow.

3. Boston has many homes schools and businesses.

4. Boston New York and Philadelphia are three of the oldest American cities.

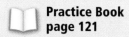

Practice Book page 121

Write a Persuasive Letter

When you write a persuasive letter, give evidence from real life. You can also use newspaper and library sources. That will help others see your point. Read how Thomas and Allison gave evidence to support their idea.

To Principal Hughes:

    The students at Webster School want more art classes. Art skills are important. They will help us get good jobs in the future. Research shows that people look at more T.V. commercials, signs, and ads than ever before. As a result, marketing and advertising may be important careers when we grow up. We need to be prepared. We hope the school board will consider our idea.

Respectfully,
Thomas Beck and Allison Ventner

SPELLING TIP

Add *-er* to a word to mean "more," as in *fast* and *faster*. When a word ends in silent *e*, you only need to add *-r*, as in *fine* and *finer*.

Practice Book page 122

Practice

Write a persuasive letter.

- Think of something you care about. Decide who your audience is.
- Decide what you want to persuade them about.
- Make your point clear. Be sure to give evidence to support it.

Writing Checklist

✓ Did you address your letter to someone who can help?

✓ Did you include evidence to support your idea?

✓ Can a partner understand your idea?

Living in the Trees

Vocabulary

Living in the Trees is about treehouses.

Key Words

- nest
- amenities
- comforts
- structures
- natural

Words in Context

1 My sisters like to **nest** in bed when they read. The blankets and pillows feel nice and warm.

2 Travelers choose hotels for **amenities**, such as nice beds or televisions. They want all the **comforts** of home.

3 People live in many kinds of **structures**. Most people live in homes or apartment buildings. In some places, people live on houseboats.

4 Some people live in houses made of human-made materials, such as bricks, cement, glass, and steel. Other people live in houses made from **natural** materials, such as tree branches or dried mud. What is your house made of?

Practice

Use each key word in a sentence.

Make Connections

What kind of shelter do you live in? Would you like to live in a teepee, an igloo, a treehouse, or a houseboat? What do you think that shelter would be like?

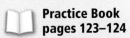

Practice Book pages 123–124

FUNCTIONAL WRITING

Student Report

?

The **Big** Question

Why do you think some people might like to live in treehouses?

Reading Strategy

Visualize

- As you read, look for words that describe people, places, and things.
- Use the words to help you create a picture in your mind.

Living in the Trees

by Ramona Vasquez

Many people live high in the air. I have a friend who lives in an apartment building. She lives on the seventh floor. I have another friend who lives in a big, old house. His bedroom is up in the attic. But did you know that some people live up in the trees?

---

attic   space in a building just under the roof

This large treehouse is in my neighbor's woods.

Most treehouses are made for children to play in.

Most of us know what treehouses are. Usually they are simple structures built in trees. They are made by securing a few wood boards to strong tree branches. You climb trees or ladders to get to them.

This kind of treehouse is found in many backyards. Perhaps you have even been in one.

Treehouses are fun places for play or rest. But would you want to live in one? Lots of people do!

---

securing firmly attaching

CheckUp Where is an attic located?

249

Stairs connect the rooms of this treehouse in California.

This treehouse is in a jungle in Indonesia.

A treehouse can be a real home. Some have walls and a roof. They also might have a door and windows. These treehouses protect people from the weather.

Many native peoples around the world live in treehouses. They have lived in these structures for generations. Some people in the United States live in treehouses, too. Their treehouses have all the comforts and amenities of an apartment or a house on a street.

---

generations   the period of time between a person's birth and the birth of that person's children

native   people who were the first to live in a place

A woman in Tahiti reads in her treehouse.

Most people are happy with their home on the ground. Other people are happy to live up high in the sky.

I think houses in the trees help people feel closer to the natural world. They let people nest high in the sky. Like birds, treehouse dwellers have a happy home in the trees

---

dwellers   person or animal that lives in a place

Practice Book
pages 125–126

Reading Strategy

Visualize

As you read this selection, you were asked to visualize.

- What did you visualize as you read?
- Did visualizing help you understand the selection? How?

Think It Over

1. What is this selection about?

2. Why do people build treehouses?

3. What do you think it is like to live in a treehouse?

251

Phonics & Fluency

Phonics

R-Controlled: *ar, or, ore*

Read each pair of words. Notice how the letter *r* changes the vowel sound.

am	ton	toe
arm	torn	tore

Here are more words with an *r* that follows a vowel.

art	for
hard	California
garden	more

Rule Box

The letters *ar* usually have the vowel sound in **art**. The letters *or* and *ore* usually have the vowel sound in **torn** and **tore**.

Practice

Read each pair of words with a partner.

• Tell whether the words have the same vowel sound.

1. bark, yard

2. port, park

3. part, pat

4. hose, horse

Fluency

Read for Speed and Accuracy

You should read quickly. But never read so quickly
that you lose your understanding.

Practice

Read for one minute.	Count the words you read.	Study any hard words.	Read and count again.

Most of us know what treehouses are. Usually they are	10
simple structures built in trees. They are made by securing	20
a few wood boards to strong tree branches. You climb trees	31
or ladders to get to them.	37
This kind of treehouse is found in many backyards.	46
Perhaps you have even been in one.	53
Treehouses are fun places for play or rest. But would	63
you want to live in one? Lots of people do!	73
A treehouse can be a real home. Some have walls and	84
a roof. They also might have a door and windows. These	95
treehouses protect people from the weather.	101
Many native peoples around the world live in	109
treehouses. They have lived in these structures for	117
generations. Some people in the United States live in	126
treehouses, too. Their treehouses have all the comforts	134
and amenities of an apartment or a house on a street.	145

Comprehension

Visualize

When you read, try to **visualize**, or picture in your mind, what the author is describing. Authors use words to draw word pictures. This helps readers create mind pictures.

Learning Strategy

Summarize

Summarize the selection for a partner.

? Ask your partner to respond to the Big Question for this reading.

Practice

What picture do you see in your mind when you read each sentence? Choose one sentence and draw what you see.

1. People can make treehouses in backyards. They must secure wooden boards to strong tree branches.

2. Some people build treehouses high in the jungle.

3. Some treehouses have many rooms. They even have staircases.

4. People who live in treehouses nest high in the sky with the birds.

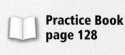

Practice Book page 128

Use an Organizational Chart

An Organizational Chart helps you put your thoughts in order. Suppose you want a friend to picture the different treehouses that you read about. The chart will help you think of ways to describe treehouses.

Practice

Copy and complete this chart. Then answer the questions.

1. Describe to a partner one of the treehouses you added to your chart.

2. How did the Organizational Chart help you describe that treehouse?

3. Which treehouse from the selection would you like to visit? Explain.

4. Would you like to live in a treehouse? Tell why or why not.

Kind of Treehouse	How It Looks	How It Is Used
simple treehouse	wooden boards attached to branches	for play or rest

Extension

Suppose you could design your own treehouse. Draw or describe it. Share your design with your class.

255

Grammar & Writing

Adjectives and Articles

An **adjective** can describe a noun.

> In these sentences, the adjectives are shown in red. The nouns they describe are shown in blue.
>
> Treehouses are **simple** structures.
>
> They rest on **strong** branches.

The words ***the, a,*** and ***an*** are called **articles**. These special adjectives point out nouns.

> In these sentences, the articles are shown in red. The nouns they refer to are shown in blue.
>
> Treehouse dwellers have **a** home in **the** tall trees.
>
> That treehouse has **an** entrance.

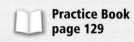

**Practice Book
page 129**

Practice

Copy each sentence. Draw one line under each adjective. Draw two lines under each article.

1. My family is building an amazing treehouse.

2. Mom bought long boards at the store.

3. Dad attached them to strong branches on the tree.

4. Soon we will build the walls and a roof.

Write a Persuasive Speech

When you **persuade** people, you get them to think or act in a way that you want. In this speech, Toby is trying to persuade people to help fix traffic problems.

> Every morning in Bellevue, our streets are dangerous. They are crowded with traffic. The school bus moves very slowly. It is hard for people to cross the street. Students at my school have an idea. We think one-way streets would help traffic move more smoothly. We think something should be done right away!

Practice

Write a short persuasive speech.

1. Find a subject. Think about something that is important to your school, home, or community.

2. Write your main idea clearly.

3. Add evidence to persuade your audience. Find facts from sources you can trust.

4. Add humor or personal feelings to make your speech stronger.

SPELLING TIP

Divide a word into syllables to help you spell it.

un / der / neath
sum / mer
com / fort

Practice Book
page 130

Writing Checklist

✓ Did you make your opinions or feelings clear?

✓ Did you use humor or emotion to make your speech stronger?

✓ Did you use evidence to help persuade your audience?

✓ Can a partner understand your speech? Did you persuade your partner?

Life at the Top of the World

by Haruki Tokama

Fur clothing keeps the Inuit people warm.

The Arctic is located, or found, at the top of the world. It is the area around the North Pole. The weather is cold there because ice covers the ground.

Parts of many places make up this area. Pieces of Russia, Alaska, Canada, and Greenland form the Arctic.

The Arctic is at the top of the globe.

The Inuit people have lived in the Arctic for a long time. Their name means "the people."

Today, most Inuit live in houses made of wood. The Inuit are known for another kind of shelter, too. It is called an igloo. Hard snow and ice form its walls.

Most Inuit now live in houses such as this one.

An igloo is a house made from blocks of snow or ice.

Today, snowmobiles take people from place to place.

Life is not always easy in the Arctic. Most people live in towns along the icy coast. Many people fish for food. Some hunt sea animals, such as whales, walruses, and seals. Others hunt caribou, bears, and smaller animals on the land.

Long ago, the Inuit followed the animals they hunted. They used boats in summer. They used sleds in winter. Dogs pulled those sleds.

Today, the Inuit stay mostly in their towns. But they still travel. They use kayaks in the waters of the Arctic. Many people also ride snowmobiles, which are sleds with motors.

Some Inuit travel by kayak.

The Inuit use every part of the animals they hunt.

Long ago, the first Inuit people came to the Arctic. They had to adapt. That means they learned to live in the area. As they adapted, this cold place became comfortable, or felt nice, to them.

The Inuit people are proud of their traditions. Some still build igloos. Some still make clothing and tools from animal skins and bones. Many still like to hunt and fish in the old ways. The Inuit have been doing these things for a long time.

Most Inuit would never want to leave the Arctic. It is their home.

Inuit children play with friends outside.

UNIT 5 Wrap Up

The Big Question

What is it like to live in an unusual home?

Written	**Oral**	**Visual/Active**
Journal Entry	**Description**	**Illustration**
Imagine you live in one of the houses you read about. Write a journal entry describing a day in your life. Include many specific details.	Describe one of the houses you read about. Give details, but do not identify the kind of house. Have listeners guess which house you are describing.	Choose one of the houses you read about. Create your own illustration of that house. Use the illustrations in your book as a guide.
Materials List	**Dedication Speech**	**Treehouse Design**
Think of a special kind of house that you would like to build. Write a list of materials that you would need to build the house.	Imagine you just built a new house. Deliver a speech about this house. Use a house you read about or imagine one of your own.	Look at the treehouses you read about. Think of a treehouse you would like to build. Draw a design for it.
Building Proposal	**Interview**	**Charades**
Imagine a new kind of house. Write a proposal for building that house. Tell why your house would be special.	Interview someone who lives in a different kind of house than you. Ask about the good and bad parts of living in that house. Record your interview.	Choose a house you read about. Act out a daily activity in that house. Have other students guess which house you are living in. Act out living in other houses.

262

✔ Learning Checklist

Word Analysis and Phonics

✓ Identify homophones.

✓ Identify *y* as a vowel.

✓ Identify *r*-controlled words with *ar*, *or*, and *ore*.

Comprehension

✓ Know the difference between facts and opinions.

✓ Use a Fact and Opinion Chart.

✓ Identify author's purpose.

✓ Use a Compare and Contrast Chart.

✓ Visualize when reading.

✓ Create an Organizational Chart.

Grammar and Writing

✓ Use commas in place names and dates.

✓ Use commas in a series.

✓ Recognize and use adjectives and articles.

✓ Write a brochure.

✓ Write a persuasive letter.

✓ Write a persuasive speech.

Self-Evaluation Questions

- How has your work improved over time?

- What will you do differently next time you write?

- How does what you've learned relate to the future?

UNIT 6
Links to Our Past

Do you ever think about the past? Stories about the past can help you learn about or remember life long ago.

READINGS

1

The Moon Tree

2

Life on the Frontier

3

A Hike Back in Time

The Big Question

What was life like in the past and why should we learn about it?

LISTENING AND SPEAKING

You will talk about what you would like to remember from your past.

WRITING

You will write a rhyme comparing your life with the lives of your parents.

Bonus Reading

The History of Money

Quick Write

Did anyone in your family come from another country? Describe something you know about another country's past.

What Do You Know about the Past?

Words to Know

1. Use these words to talk about studying the past.

 photographs

 journals

 museum

 cave paintings

 fossils

---

2. How can you learn about the past?

To learn about the past, I can look _____ .

 at photographs

 at cave paintings

 in journals

 at fossils

 in a museum

3. What do you study to learn about the past?

I study _____ to learn about _____ .

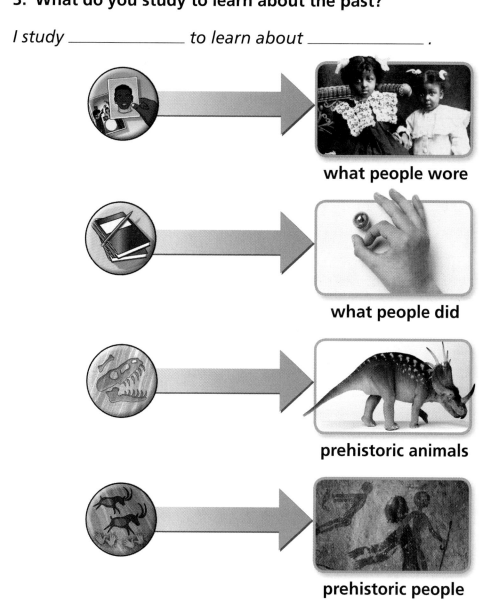

what people wore

what people did

prehistoric animals

prehistoric people

4. Use these words to talk about how the past was different.

transportation

education

entertainment

communication

Your Stories about Links to the Past

France

India

Marie-Paule

I live in France. I like to visit caves where people lived long ago. You can see tools and clothing that prehistoric people used. Many of the caves have paintings on the walls. Ancient people painted objects and animals that were important to them.

Rajan

I live in India. There are many weavers in my country. They use colorful wool yarns to make beautiful fabric. Many of the patterns are hundreds of years old. They have been passed down through generations.

Washington, D.C.
U.S.A.

Mexico

Jacob

I live in Washington, D.C. That is the capital of the United States. My mom works for the United States Mint. That is where American money is printed. Mom says we can learn a lot about a country's past by looking at its money. George Washington's picture is on our dollar bill. He was our first president.

Alicia

I live in Mexico. My favorite day is September 16th. That is the day Mexico became free from Spain. Every year, my country celebrates its birthday. We dress in special clothes on that day. We also sing special songs that celebrate our past.

What about you?

1 What would you like to save to help you remember your past?

2 How are these students' stories similar to yours?

3 What are some ways that your family celebrates the past? Tell your story!

269

The Moon Tree

Key Words

signatures

mission

astronaut

plaque

explorer

surrounded

Vocabulary

***The Moon Tree* tells about two boys who try to save an important tree.**

Words in Context

1 Some people wanted a park in the city. They asked everyone to sign a form. They needed as many **signatures** as possible.

2 The *Apollo 11* space **mission** was the first time a human landed on the moon. Scientists worked for many years to make the mission a success.

3 An **astronaut** must wear a spacesuit to go outside of the space shuttle.

4 The team got a **plaque** after winning the championship.

5 The **explorer** looked for signs of an old city. He searched deep in the jungle.

6 The statue is **surrounded** by pretty flowers.

Practice

Use each key word in a sentence.

Make Connections

Some buildings have plaques telling about a famous person who lived there. Imagine a plaque on the place where you live. What would it say about you?

Academic Words

occur
happen

justify
give a good reason for

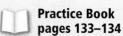

Practice Book pages 133–134

271

LITERATURE

Realistic Fiction

The **Big** Question

Why is it important for people to save things from the past?

Reading Strategy

Identify Problem and Solution

- As you read, think about the problems the characters face.

- Keep reading to find the solutions to the problems.

The Moon Tree

by Dan Ahearn
illustrated by Lee White

The ball flew like a rocket into the woods. Hector found the ball next to a strange, flat stone. The stone was dirty and scratched. It rested against a tall sycamore tree. On the stone was a brass plaque. It said:

The seed of this tree was a space explorer.
It went to the moon
with the crew of the Apollo 14.
The seed was planted here on July 4, 1976.

Hector ran to get his friend Stuart. He didn't notice the red flags that circled the tree.

---

sycamore   North American tree with broad leaves

crew   people who work together

Apollo 14   third spaceship to land on the moon

CheckUp   **What did Hector find when he was looking for a ball?**

Hector and Stuart ran to the library. They read about the moon trees. The boys learned that 500 seeds went on the space mission. The seeds didn't land on the moon. They stayed in orbit with astronaut Stuart Roosa. It had been his idea to bring the seeds.

Back on Earth, the seeds grew into normal trees. Space travel had not changed them. People planted hundreds of moon tree seedlings. The trees grew all over the world.

The boys told the librarian, Mrs. Wu, about the moon tree.

---

orbit   a path in space made when one thing moves around a larger thing

seedlings   young plants grown from seeds

"I forgot about our moon tree," said Mrs. Wu. "But I have bad news." She explained that most of the woods would be gone soon. Stakes with red flags surrounded each tree that would be cut down.

"Why?" cried Hector.

"To make room for the new shopping mall," said Mrs. Wu.

"That's not right," said Stuart. "There must be something we can do!"

Mrs. Wu said they needed a plan. She and the boys talked all day about how to save the moon tree. By the time the library closed, they had a plan.

---

stakes pointed objects stuck in the ground to mark places

Check Up What problem did the boys discover?

The boys met with their friends. They told their friends the plan to save the moon tree.

Hector held up a paper. "This is a petition," he said. "It says, 'The moon tree is an important part of history. It is too valuable to lose. Please spare our moon tree.' We need everybody in town to sign this petition."

"Signatures will show that people care," Stuart said. "We need a lot of signatures. Then the builders might not cut down the moon tree."

Hector said, "Ask everybody to sign the petition! Save the moon tree!"

---

petition   written request signed by a lot of people

spare   save or not damage

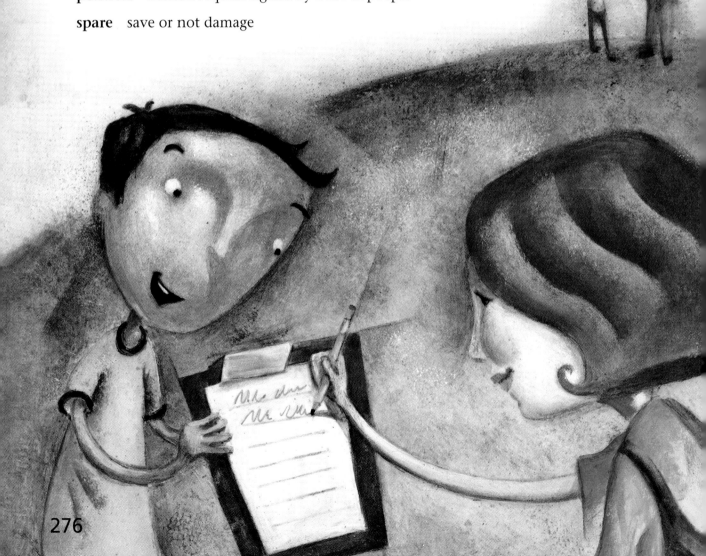

They called themselves the Moon Tree Crew. Then Stuart named the tree. He said, "Our moon tree needs a name. People will care more about a tree called . . . Apollo."

Stuart knew about these things. His father worked in the advertising business.

Mrs. Wu made posters. Each poster had a slogan: "Save Apollo, the moon tree."

The boys and their friends were busy. Some went to stores. Others walked down Main Street. They told people the moon tree's story. The whole town wanted to help. The Moon Tree Crew got hundreds of signatures.

---

advertising business that tells people about a product

slogan short phrase that is easy to remember

CheckUp How did going to the library lead to a solution?

Hector and Stuart took the petition to Mr. Bowman. He built shopping malls for a living.

"Boys, you've made this tree famous," he said. "How did you do it?"

"My father told me how," said Stuart. "He works in advertising."

Mr. Bowman laughed. "When I was your age, I saw the first lunar landing on TV. But has this tree really been to the moon?"

"Yes, but it was only a seed then," said Hector.

"It never actually landed on the moon," Stuart added. "It only orbited the moon."

Mr. Bowman was silent for a moment. "That's close enough for me," he said.

---

living   way to earn money

lunar   about the moon

orbited   traveled in a circle in space around a larger thing

Mr. Bowman did build a shopping mall. But he saved Apollo, the moon tree. He had the old plaque cleaned and shined. Under the old plaque, he added a new one. It said:

The Moon Tree Crew saved this tree.

"Thank you!" said Hector and Stuart.

"No, thank *you*," said Mr. Bowman. "This tree brings all of us closer to the moon."

Practice Book
pages 135–136

Reading Strategy

Identify Problem and Solution

- What problems did the boys in the story have?
- How did they solve the problems?
- Did thinking about the problems and solutions help you understand this story? How?

Think It Over

1. What was the moon tree?

2. How did the boys learn about this special tree?

3. Why was the moon tree in danger?

279

Phonics & Fluency

Phonics

Diphthongs: *ow, ou*

Notice the vowel sounds in these words.

how	loud	low

Which words have the same letters?
Which words have the same vowel sound?

- The letters *ow* and *ou* can have the vowel sound you hear in **how** and **loud**.
- The letters *ow* can also have the long *o* sound you hear in **low**.

Rule Box

The words **how** and **loud** have the same sound, but the *ow* sound is spelled differently. The words **how** and **low** have the same *ow* spelling, but different sounds.

Practice

Read the words below with a partner.

1. List the words in which *ow* or *ou* has the vowel sound in **how**.

2. List the words in which *ow* has the long *o* sound in **low**.

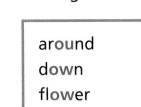

around	how	show
down	know	south
flower	out	tomorrow

Fluency

Look Ahead

Sometimes, readers look for hard words before they read. They then try to figure them out.

| Pick one passage. | Find any hard words. | Practice saying those words. | Read the passage aloud. |

1 Two boys find a special tree marked by a plaque. The tree is going to be cut down. The boys start a campaign to save the tree.

2 Each poster had a slogan: "Save Apollo, the moon tree."
The boys and their friends were busy. Some went to stores. Others walked down Main Street. They told people the moon tree's story. The whole town wanted to help. The Moon Tree Crew got hundreds of signatures.

3 "It never actually landed on the moon," Stuart added. "It only orbited the moon."
Mr. Bowman was silent for a moment. "That's close enough for me," he said.
Mr. Bowman did build his shopping mall. But he saved Apollo the moon tree. He had the old plaque cleaned and shined. Under the old plaque, he added a new one. It said:
The Moon Tree Crew saved this tree.

Comprehension

Problem and Solution

Problems and solutions make a story more interesting. A **problem** is a conflict that characters have. The **solution** is how characters solve, or fix, the problem. There can be more than one problem and solution in a story.

As you read, ask yourself:

- "What is the main, or most important, conflict?"
- "What does the main character want?"

Learning Strategy

Outline

Make an outline of the main characters and events in the story.

Share your outline with a partner.

? Ask your partner to respond to the Big Question for this reading.

Practice

Write the solution to each problem. The first one is done for you.

Problem	Solution
1. Hector and Stuart wanted to learn about moon trees.	1. Hector and Stuart went to the library to read about moon trees.
2. Hector, Stuart, and Mrs. Wu wanted to save the tree.	2.
3. Hector, Stuart, and Mrs. Wu wanted people to know about their plan.	3.
4. Mr. Bowman wanted to build a new shopping mall.	4.

Practice Book

📖

page 138

Use a Problem and Solution Chart

A Problem and Solution Chart can help you record problems and solutions in a story.

Practice

Copy this chart. Then reread *The Moon Tree*. Write about the main problem and its solution.

Problem

Who? _____

What? _____

Why? _____

↓

Solution

Who? _____

What? _____

Why? _____

↓

Results

_____

_____

_____

Extension

If you were with Hector and Stuart, what would you have done? How would you have solved the problem? Make a drawing or act out a scene. Show your idea to the class.

Grammar & Writing

The Verbs *Be* and *Go*

Be and *go* are both **irregular verbs**. You do not form the past tense by adding -*ed*.

Be		
Subject	**Present Tense**	**Past Tense**
I	am	was
he, she, it, Hector	is	was
you, we, they, boys	are	were

Go		
Subject	**Present Tense**	**Past Tense**
I	go	went
he, she, it, Hector	goes	went
you, we, they, boys	go	went

Practice

Write each sentence. Use the correct form of the verb.

1. Hector _____ to the library with Stuart. (*go*—past)

2. The two boys ____ friends. (*be*—present)

3. Mrs. Wu _____ very helpful. (*be*—past)

4. The seeds _____ into space. (*go*—past)

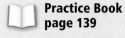

Practice Book page 139

284

Write a Compare and Contrast Paragraph

It's easy to compare and contrast two things if you make a chart first. Nigella made a chart before comparing baseball and soccer.

Baseball	Soccer
1. Baseball is fun to play.	1. Soccer is fun to play.
2. You use a glove and a bat.	2. You kick the ball with your feet. You can use your head but not your hands.
3. Players take turns.	3. Players run all the time.
4. Sometimes, players must wait a long time.	4. There's a lot of action for every player.

Baseball and soccer are both fun, but they are very different. In baseball, you catch a ball with a glove. You hit the ball with a bat. In soccer, you kick the ball with your feet. You can use your head, too, but not your hands. In baseball, players take turns batting and running to the bases. Sometimes they wait a long time. In soccer, players run all the time. I like soccer best because there is more action for every player.

SPELLING TIP

The letters *gh* are sometimes silent as in **high**, **light**, and **straight**. Notice words with silent *gh* and learn their spellings.

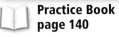

Practice Book page 140

Practice

Make a chart to compare and contrast two places you want to visit. Then write a paragraph to compare and contrast those places.

Writing Checklist

✓ Did your paragraph compare or contrast two places?

✓ Did you write a conclusion?

✓ Can a partner understand your description?

285

Life on the Frontier

Vocabulary

Life on the Frontier is a song about a family that lives on the frontier.

Words in Context

1 The wood carver took **pride** in his work. He wanted everything he made to be perfect.

2 **Objects** are anything you can touch. How are all these objects related?

3 Some things are **valuable** because they cost a lot of money. Other things are valuable because someone loves them.

Key Words

pride

objects

valuable

memories

treasures

roam

286

4 Photographs bring back **memories**. They help people remember things that happened.

5 To me, the teddy bear and blanket are not special. To Rocco, they are his most loved **treasures**.

6 My family likes to take long walks. Every weekend, we **roam** in the woods for hours.

Practice

Use each key word in a sentence.

Make Connections

Think of some things that are valuable and cost a lot of money. Now think of some things that are valuable but are not worth much money. Tell about something that is valuable to you but can not be bought.

Academic Words

aware
know about

reject
not accept

📖 **Practice Book**
pages 141–142

287

The Big Question

Why do people write songs and stories about the past?

Reading Strategy

Summarize

A summary of a piece tells the main ideas.

- Read this song.
- Notice the main ideas.

Life on the Frontier

by Rachel Marie Lee
illustrated by Diana Kizlauskas

Sung to the tune of "Yankee Doodle Dandy"

I'm a pioneer with much pride
And many memories, as well.
From Pennsylvania into Oregon,
Here's where I happily dwell.

I came with valuable objects:
Tools, Ma's books, and our dog, Sam.
Now I have some brand new treasures.
One's the farmland I roam
With my new sister, Pam.

---

dwell   live in a place

A log cabin is our new home.
We rise at dawn to do the chores.
With a tap, tap, tap, then a cut, cut, cut,
Pa chops the logs and makes doors.

It isn't all work and no fun, though.
Pa likes to play his banjo.
Ma will sing. I'll dance a jig.
And little Pam will smile.
We're happy in our new frontier home.

---

dawn   beginning of the day when light first appears

chores   jobs that are done around the house

jig   fast, lively dance

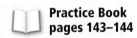
**Practice Book
pages 143–144**

Reading Strategy

Summarize

- What is this song about?
- In your own words, summarize the song.
- Did summarizing help you understand the song? How?

Think It Over

1 Who is the narrator of this song?

2 Where does he live?

3 What does his father do?

4 How does this family entertain themselves at night?

The American Frontier

◀ **Frontier trade**
Many European explorers traded with Native Americans on the frontier.

Famous frontiersman ▶
Davy Crockett was a hunter, soldier, and politician on the frontier.

▲ **Log cabin**
Many people on the frontier lived in log cabins.

◄ Wilderness guide

Sacajawea was a Shoshone guide who helped Meriwether Lewis and William Clark.

▲ Famous explorers

Lewis and Clark were the first people to travel over land to the Pacific coast and back.

Compass ►

Equipment such as this compass helped explorers travel west.

Activity to Do!

These two pages use pictures and words to tell about the American frontier.

- Imagine you lived when the American west was a frontier.
- What do you think it was like?
- Write a two-page story about a day on the frontier. Draw pictures for your story.

Word Analysis & Fluency

Word Analysis
Compound Words

Sometimes, two words come together to form a new word. These new words are called **compound words**.

> farm + land = **farmland**   night + time = **nighttime**

Rule Box

Look for the smaller words that make up a compound word. They can help you pronounce the compound word.

Smaller words in a compound word also help you understand the meaning of the larger word. For example, *farmland* is land used for farming.

Practice

- Read the clues below.
- Choose a word from each box to form a compound word to match each clue.

back	time
day	fall
news	yard
water	paper

1. This is the time when it is day.

2. This is water that falls from a high place.

3. This is news printed on sheets of paper.

4. This is a yard in back of a house.

Fluency

Read with Expression

When you read aloud, use your voice to show feelings.

Practice

| Read silently. | Read aloud. | Get comments. | Read aloud again. |

A log cabin is our new home.
We rise at dawn to do the chores.
With a tap, tap, tap, then a cut, cut, cut,
Pa chops the logs and makes doors.

It isn't all work and no fun, though.
Pa likes to play his old banjo.
Ma will sing. I'll dance a jig.
And little Pam will smile.
We're happy in our new frontier home.

Comprehension

Summarize

When you **summarize**, you retell the main ideas and details of a story. The main idea and the details are the most important parts of a story.

- Ask yourself **who**, **what**, **where**, **when**, and **why** questions to find the main idea of a story.
- Look for details that support the main idea.

Practice

Reread *Life on the Frontier*. Look at the pictures. Then answer the questions to complete the Details column.

Questions About the Main Idea	Details
1. **Who** is the song about?	1. a family living on the American frontier
2. **What** is the song about?	2.
3. **Where** does the family come from?	3.
4. **When** does the poem take place?	4.
5. **Why** is the pioneer family happy?	5.

Practice Book page 146

Use a Main Idea and Details Chart

A Main Idea and Details Chart helps you record the main idea and most important details as you read.

Practice

Use the chart on the previous page to help you find the main idea of the song. Then list three details that support that idea.

The main idea is:
_____
_____

Detail
_____
_____
_____
_____

Detail
_____
_____
_____
_____

Detail
_____
_____
_____
_____

Grammar & Writing

Possessive Nouns and Adjectives

Possessives are words that show ownership.
Possessive nouns are formed from nouns. They have apostrophes. They can be singular or plural.

Rules	Examples
To make a **singular noun** possessive, add an apostrophe (') and s.	mother ⟶ mother's pioneer ⟶ pioneer's
To make a **plural noun** that ends in s possessive, just add an apostrophe.	boys ⟶ boys' pioneers ⟶ pioneers'

Possessive adjectives also show ownership. They can be singular or plural.

Singular Possessive Adjectives	Plural Possessive Adjectives
my home *your* home *his, her, its* home	*our* home *your* home *their* home

Practice

List each possessive noun and possessive adjective.

1. We came to Oregon with our dog and Pa's banjo.

2. Everyone wanted to hear the girls' stories.

3. They told about their long journey to your country.

Write a Poem or Song

Read the short poem Tamara wrote. She used the tune "Eensy Weensy Spider" to help her with the rhythm.

> When my dad was ten,
> There wasn't too much fun.
> They had no videos.
> And CDs? There were none.
>
> When my dad was ten,
> There wasn't a cell phone.
> He didn't use computers,
> And the Web then was unknown.

Practice

Write a poem about how life was different when your parents were children.

Sometimes, thinking of a song helps you find a rhythm for a poem. Poems don't always need to rhyme, but it makes them more fun to listen to. Put rhymes in your poem.

Practice Book page 148

SPELLING TIP

At the end of a word, the sound /j/ can be spelled *-ge* or *-dge*.

- If a long vowel comes before /j/, use *-ge*: **cage**, **huge**.

- If a consonant comes before /j/, use *-ge*: **change**, **urge**.

- If a short vowel comes before /j/, use *-dge*: **badge**, **hedge**.

Writing Checklist

✔ Did you write about how life is different now?

✔ Did you use rhyming words?

✔ Can a partner understand your poem?

A Hike Back in Time

Vocabulary

A Hike Back in Time is about a girl who visits the Grand Canyon.

Key Words

- thrive
- hiking
- trails
- thrilling
- canyon
- ledge

Words in Context

1 Plants need water to grow and **thrive**. Which plant do you think gets more water?

2 **Hiking** is a lot of fun. You don't need a bike or a car. You just walk on **trails** that go up the mountain.

3 The rides at the fair are **thrilling**! They are scary and fun at the same time.

4 The **canyon** was deep and wide.

5 The skier stopped to look over the **ledge** of the mountain.

Practice

Use each key word in a sentence.

Make Connections

Have you been on a hike? Where did you go? If you have not been on a hike, where would you like to go? Why?

Academic Words

pursue

chase or follow

area

place or location

 Practice Book
pages 149–150

LITERATURE

Realistic Fiction

The Big Question

How do some places help people think about the past?

Reading Strategy

Identify Plot and Setting

- The plot is what happens in a story.
- The setting is where a story takes place.
- Picture the plot and the setting in your mind as you read.

A Hike Back in Time

by Pam Walker
illustrated by Tom Newsom

Last year, I went to the Grand Canyon for the first time. I wanted to walk the same paths my grandmother walked many years ago. I wanted to see the same sights she saw. As I followed in her footsteps, I felt like I was taking a trip back in time!

---

sights   things someone can see, often things that are beautiful or unusual

footsteps   same path that someone took before

I never knew my grandmother, but I have a picture of her. She is standing in front of a waterfall.

On our first day, my parents and I paused at a ledge. We looked down into the deep canyon. "I wonder if that's the trail to the waterfall," I said.

The desert colors were beautiful. I loved the shades of browns, greens, and yellows. I wondered what my grandmother had thought when she looked across the canyon. Had the sun warmed her face the way it warmed mine?

---

waterfall   water that falls down over a cliff

paused   stopped for a short time

shades   darkness and lightness of colors

CheckUp ▶ In the canyon, the girl thinks of her grandmother. Why?

We walked for a long time along the trail, but we didn't find the waterfall. As the sun rose higher in the sky, we put on hats to shade our faces.

My dad said, "Maybe we should turn back and get a fresh start tomorrow."

Then I saw a sign. "Supai!" I said. "That's the village I read about. Maybe somebody there knows about the waterfall."

"What do you think?" my dad asked my mom.

"Well, we've come this far," Mom said. "I think we should keep going."

"On to Supai!" I cried.

---

shade   protect from direct light

fresh   new

In Supai, we met an old man who worked at a store. I asked if I could take his picture for my scrapbook.

Then I showed him the picture of my grandmother. He smiled when he looked at the picture. He said that my grandmother had a kind face.

"I want to find the same waterfall," I told him. "I want to see all the things my grandmother saw."

"That's Mooney Falls," he said. "Stay at the lodge tonight and go there in the morning."

"Can we, Dad?" I asked. "Can we, Mom?"

"Well, we've come this far," they said.

---

scrapbook   book to store or other things you want to keep

lodge   hotel away from the city

Check Up   Why does the girl want to go to Mooney Falls?

I was so excited about hiking to Mooney Falls, I was afraid I wouldn't sleep. But I did sleep. Our long hike had made me tired. I fell asleep right away.

When I opened my eyes the next morning, my dad was already awake.

"Let's go!" he said. "We have an appointment with Mooney Falls, remember?"

"Not so fast," said Mom. "First, we need to get some supplies."

We returned to the store and bought some water, a compass, and a trail map.

"Ready, Mom?" I asked impatiently.

"Ready," she said. "Now we're equipped for a long day on the trails."

---

appointment   meeting at a certain time and place

impatiently   not wanting to wait

equipped   have the things needed to do something

"Hold on to the chain!" Mom said.

"Watch your step!" Dad said.

We hiked deeper and deeper into the canyon. Each trail was more thrilling than the last.

"I'm glad we bought the trail map," I said. "Supai seems so far away."

Mom smiled. "I know how much you want to find Mooney Falls," she said. "I want to find it, too."

"Do you think Grandmother used a trail map?" I asked.

"No," Mom said. "My mother knew this canyon. It was like her own backyard. She could thrive in the wilderness."

"Shhh," Dad said. "I hear something."

---

chain   metal rings connected together in a line

wilderness   large land area that humans have not changed

CheckUp ▶ Do you think the canyon was important to the girl's grandmother?

We heard the faint sound of water in the distance. As we walked, the noise got louder. The air felt cooler. Then we turned a corner, and the trail stopped. I saw a tall waterfall pouring into a clear pool.

"Mooney Falls!" I cried.

I glanced at my grandmother's picture. "It looks just like it did fifty years ago."

I dipped my hand into the cool water and let it pour through my fingers. I wondered if my grandmother had done the same thing.

"We should go back," Dad said. "But first, we need a picture."

---

faint   hard to hear

glanced   quickly looked at

I stood in front of the waterfall while Dad pulled the camera out of his bag.

"Wait a second," Mom said. She picked up a stick from the side of the trail. "You need a walking stick. Now, you look just like your grandmother."

I looked at the picture again and then held it up. "Grandmother and I are visiting the waterfall together!"

---

second very short period of time.

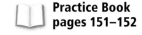
Practice Book pages 151–152

Practice Book pages 151–152

Reading Strategy

Identify Plot and Setting

- What is the plot of this story?
- What is the setting of this story?
- Did thinking about the plot and setting help you understand this story? How?

Think It Over

1 Who are the characters in this story?

2 Where are the characters going?

3 Why is Mooney Falls important?

4 How is the narrator like her grandmother?

Phonics & Fluency

Phonics

Variant Vowel: *oo*

Notice that each word is spelled with the letters *oo*.

Words with Letters *oo*	
book	too
wood	proof
foot	room

Rule Box

Sometimes the letters *oo* have the sound you hear in **took**.
Sometimes the letters *oo* have the sound you hear in **soon**.

Practice

Read the sentences with a partner. Take turns.

- Come look at my scrapbook.
- It has pictures of the trip we took.
- We spent the afternoon walking in the woods.
- There's a pool near the waterfall.

1. List the words in which oo has the vowel sound in **took**.

2. List the words in which oo has the vowel sound in **soon**.

Fluency

Read for Speed and Accuracy

You should read quickly. But never read so quickly that you lose your understanding.

Practice

| Read for one minute. | Count the words you read. | Study any hard words. | Read and count again. |

Last year, I went to the Grand Canyon for the first time. I 13
wanted to walk the same paths my grandmother walked many 23
years ago. I wanted to see the same sights she saw. As I followed 37
in her footsteps, I felt like I was taking a trip back in time! 51

I never knew my grandmother, but I have a picture of her. 63
She is standing in front of a waterfall. 71

On our first day, my parents and I paused at a ledge. We 84
looked down into the deep canyon. "I wonder if that's the trail 96
to the waterfall," I said. 101

The desert colors were beautiful. I loved the shades of 111
browns, greens, and yellows. I wondered what my grandmother 120
had thought when she looked across the canyon. Had the sun 131
warmed her face the way it warmed mine? 139

Comprehension

Plot and Setting

The **plot** is what happens in a story or play. The **setting** is the place, date, and time when the plot happens.

- As you read, look for details that tell you where and when the events happen.

Retell

Retell the story to a partner.

 Ask your partner to respond to the Big Question for this reading.

Practice

Read the paragraph. Answer the questions about the plot and setting.

Last year, I went to the Grand Canyon for the first time. I walked the same paths my grandmother walked many years ago. I saw the same sights she saw. As I followed in her footsteps, I felt like I was taking a trip back in time!

Plot	Setting
1. What happens *first*?	4. Where does this scene happen?
2. What happens *next*?	5. When does this scene happen?
3. What happens *last*?	

 Practice Book page 154

Use a Sequence of Events Chart

A Sequence of Events Chart can help you record the main events of a story's plot.

Practice

Copy this chart. Write the major events that happen in *A Hike Back in Time*. Then write about the setting of each event.

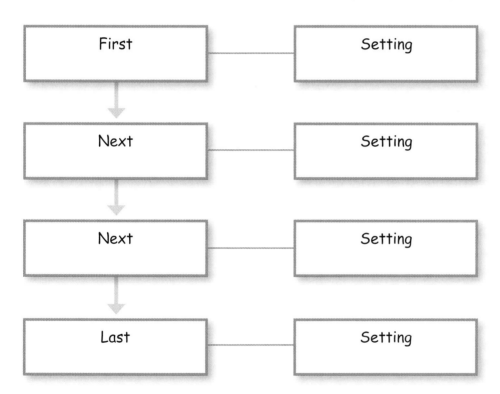

| First | Setting |

| Next | Setting |

| Next | Setting |

| Last | Setting |

Extension

Would the plot of the story change if the setting were different? Choose a new setting. Draw the scene. List plot changes. Present your new story to the class.

Grammar & Writing

Quotation Marks

Notice where the opening and closing quotation marks are placed. Also notice that in a speaker's exact words, the first word is capitalized.

Rules	Examples
When a speaker's exact words come first in a sentence, and the words are a statement, put a comma and then closing quotation marks.	"I'm glad we brought the map," I said.
When a speaker's exact words come first in a sentence, and the words are a question or exclamation, put the question mark or exclamation mark and then closing quotation marks after.	"What do you think?" my dad asked. "That looks like Supai!" I said.
When a speaker's exact words come last in a sentence, use a comma between the words that tell who is speaking and the speaker's exact words. Put the end punctuation for the exact words. Then put closing quotation marks.	My dad said, "Maybe we should turn back." My mom asked, "Is this Mooney Falls?"

Practice

Write each sentence. Use the correct punctuation.

1. Have you ever been to the Grand Canyon? Jim asked.

2. No, but I'd love to go there, I said.

3. Jim said, Let's learn more about this famous place

Practice Book page 155

Explain the Steps in a Process

To explain a process, you write the steps in order. Read the steps Yanik follows when he gets ready to go on a canoe trip.

Preparing for a Canoe Trip

1. Reserve a canoe the day before your trip. Many people go canoeing. So, you need to claim your canoe in advance.
2. Carry trail mix. This healthy snack gives you energy. Bring a towel, because you might get wet. Bring insect spray in case there are bugs.
3. Wear protective clothing. The sun can be hot. You must protect your eyes, skin, and head.
4. Bring money to rent your canoe. Wear a life jacket, because a canoe can tip over. Finally, put the canoe in the water and paddle away!

SPELLING TIP

Learn common homophones, such as *ate* and *eight*. Make sure you use the correct homophone in your writing. Check a dictionary to be sure.

Practice Book page 156

Practice

Think of something you do that has steps, such as making a sandwich. Make a list of the steps.

- Put the steps in order.
- Explain what you do in each step.

First

↓

Next

↓

Next

↓

Last

Writing Checklist

✓ Did you put the steps in order?

✓ Did you explain what you do in each step?

✓ Can a partner follow your steps?

The History of Money

by Mbeke Tsango

What is money? The answer might surprise you. Money is what people agree it is. People agree that a pen is worth a dollar, or that an apple is worth an orange.

Did you ever trade an apple for an orange at lunch? If you did, you used your fruit like money. Before money was made for the first time, people bartered, or traded for things they wanted. They traded one thing for another.

When the students traded a banana for an apple, they bartered.

314

Cows, goats, pigs, and sheep were the first currency. Later, farmers traded the things they grew.

People around the world once used shell money. This belt of shells was very valuable.

The first "money" was animals. Then, when people began to farm, they traded vegetables, fruits, and grains. But people wanted money that was easier to carry. That's why early cultures around the world used shells as currency. People agreed on the value of each shell. Then they used shells to buy or sell things. In North America, Native Americans and Europeans used shells until the 1800s.

About 3,000 years ago, people in China began using metals to make shells. Then they made coins. Slowly, metal currency spread to other countries. People made coins from gold, silver, or bronze. The coins were stamped with art or images, such as rulers' faces.

How are these Asian coins different from American coins?

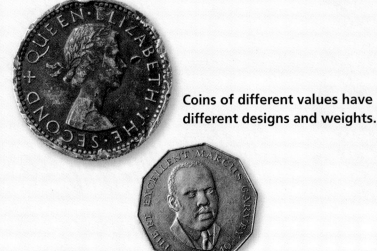

Coins of different values have different designs and weights.

At first, people weighed coins to learn their values. Later, each kind of coin got the same size, weight, and decoration.

Paper money was first made in China around A.C.E. 900. People in Europe did not use paper money until about 1650. Soon, paper money became as common as coins.

People still use paper and metal currency. But computers are changing the way we use money. Now we get money from machines. We use plastic credit cards so we can buy now and pay later. Many people now pay for things on the Internet.

Do you think we will use dollars and coins much longer?

Computers are changing the way we use money.

Currency Timeline

9000 B.C.E.	**animals**
6000 B.C.E.	**fruits and vegetables**
1200 B.C.E.	**shells**
1100 B.C.E.	**metal coins**
A.C.E. **900**	**paper money in Europe**
A.C.E. **1700**	**shells in North America**
Today	**credit cards, debit cards**
Future	**no bills or coins?**

Can you imagine a world
without coins and paper money?

The Big Question

What was life like in the past and why should we learn about it?

Written	Oral	Visual/Active
Song	**Oral Report**	**Pantomime**
Write a song about frontier life. Use a tune you like or create a new tune. Write words to tell about frontier life.	Deliver an oral report to your classmates. Tell what you learned about frontier life.	Reread the song about life on the frontier. Act out the song.
Dedication Program	**Tall Tale**	**History Cards**
Create an imaginary character who lived on the frontier. Imagine a building will be named for that person. Write a program that describes the dedication ceremony.	A tall tale stretches the facts about a person until he or she seems bigger and better than in real life. Tell your own tall tale about a person who lived on the frontier.	Research what life was like on the frontier. Create a pack of illustrated cards that show scenes from everyday life.
History Article	**Board Game**	**Park Design**
Choose an individual or event from the frontier era. Research and write a short article. Answer the 5 W questions in your article.	Create a game called *The Wild West*. Use slides for events that hurt the settlers and ladders for events that helped. Teach a group of children to play your game.	Design a frontier-life historical park. Think about what kinds of buildings and exhibits you would include. Create a map or model for the park.

✔ Learning Checklist

Word Analysis and Phonics

✓ Identify words with *ow* and *ou*.

✓ Identify compound words.

✓ Identify words with *oo*.

Comprehension

✓ Identify problems and solutions.

✓ Use a Problem and Solution Chart.

✓ Summarize a reading.

✓ Construct a Main Idea and Details Chart.

✓ Analyze plot and setting.

✓ Create a Sequence of Events Chart.

Grammar and Writing

✓ Use the verbs *be* and *go*.

✓ Form possessive nouns and pronouns.

✓ Use quotation marks.

✓ Write a compare and contrast paragraph.

✓ Write a poem or song.

✓ Write an explanation of the steps in a process.

Self-Evaluation Questions

- How difficult were the projects for you?

- What are you most proud of?

Handbook

How to Learn Language

Learning a language involves listening, speaking, reading, and writing. You can use these tips to make the most of your language learning.

LISTENING

1. Listen with a purpose.
2. Listen actively.
3. Take notes.
4. Listen to speakers on the radio, television, and Internet.

SPEAKING

1. Think before you speak.
2. Speak appropriately for your audience.
3. Practice reading aloud to a partner.
4. Practice speaking with friends and family members.
5. Remember, it is okay to make mistakes.

READING

1. Read every day.
2. Use the visuals to help you figure out what words mean.
3. Reread parts that you do not understand.
4. Read many kinds of literature.
5. Ask for help.

WRITING

1. Write something every day.
2. Plan your writing before you begin.
3. Read what you write aloud. Ask yourself whether it make sense.
4. Check for spelling and grammar mistakes.

How to Study

Here are some tips for developing good study habits.

- **Schedule a time for studying.** It is easier to develop good study habits if you set aside the same time every day to study. Once you have a study routine, it will be easier for you to find time to prepare for larger projects or tests.

- **Create a special place for studying.** Find a study area where you are comfortable and where you have everything you need for studying. If possible, choose an area that is away from telephones or television. You can play music if it helps your concentration.

- **Read the directions first.** Make sure you understand what you are supposed to do. Ask a partner or your teacher about anything you do not understand.

- **Preview the reading.** Look at the pictures, illustrations, and captions in the reading. They will help you understand the text.

- **Learn unfamiliar words.** Try to figure out what unfamiliar words mean by finding context clues in the reading. If you still can't figure out the meaning, use a dictionary.

- **Take notes.** Keep notes in a notebook or journal of important things you want to remember from the reading.

- **Ask questions.** Write any questions you have from the reading. Discuss them with a partner or your teacher.

How to Build Vocabulary

Use these ideas to help you remember the meanings of new words.

Keep a Vocabulary Notebook Keep a notebook of vocabulary words and their definitions. Test yourself by covering either the word or the definition.

Make Flashcards On the front of an index card, write a word you want to remember. On the back, write the meaning. Use the cards to review the words with a partner or family member.

Say the Words Aloud Use your new words in sentences. Say the sentences to a partner or a family member.

How to Use a Book

The Title Page The title page states the title, the author, and the publisher.

The Table of Contents The table of contents is at the front of a book. The page on which a chapter begins is next to its name.

The Glossary The glossary is a small dictionary at the back of a book. It will tell you the meaning of a word, and sometimes how to pronounce it. Use the glossary the same way you would a dictionary.

The Index The index is at the back of a book. It lists subjects and names that are in the book, along with page numbers where you can find information.

The Bibliography The bibliography at the back of a book or chapter lets you know the books or sources where an author got information.

How to Use a Dictionary and Thesaurus

The Dictionary

You can find the **spelling**, **pronunciation**, **part of speech**, and **definitions** of words in the dictionary.

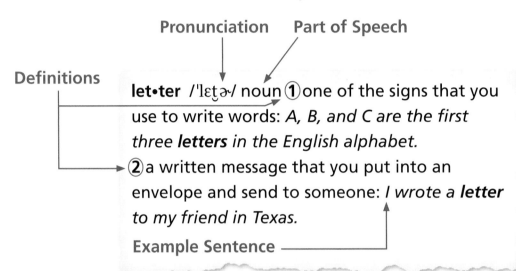

Pronunciation   Part of Speech

Definitions

let•ter /ˈlɛt̬ɚ/ noun ① one of the signs that you use to write words: *A, B, and C are the first three **letters** in the English alphabet.*

② a written message that you put into an envelope and send to someone: *I wrote a **letter** to my friend in Texas.*

Example Sentence

The Thesaurus

A thesaurus is a specialized dictionary that lists **synonyms**, or words with similar meanings, and **antonyms**, or words with opposite meanings. Words in a thesaurus are arranged alphabetically. You can look up the word just as you would look it up in a dictionary.

Main entry: sad
Part of speech: adjective[1]
Definition: unhappy
Synonyms: bitter, depressed, despairing, down, downcast, gloomy, glum, heartbroken, low, melancholy, morose, pessimistic, sorry, troubled, weeping
Antonyms: cheerful, happy

How to Take Tests

Taking tests is part of going to school. Use these tips to help you answer the kinds of questions you often see on tests.

True-False Questions

- If a statement seems true, make sure it is *all* true.
- The word *not* can change the meaning of a statement.
- Pay attention to words such as *all*, *always*, *never*, *no*, *none*, and *only*. They often make a statement false.
- Words such as *generally*, *much*, *many*, *sometimes*, and *usually* often make a statement true.

Multiple Choice Questions

- Try to answer the question before reading the choices. If your answer is one of the choices, choose it.
- Eliminate answers you know are wrong.
- Don't change your answer unless you know it is wrong.

Matching Questions

- Count each group to see whether any items will be left over.
- Read all the items before you start matching.
- Match the items you know first.

Fill-In-the-Blank Questions or Completions

- Read the question or incomplete sentence carefully.
- Look for clues in the question or sentence that might help you figure out the answer.
- If you are given possible answers, cross each out as you use it.

Short Answers and Essays

- Take a few minutes to organize your thoughts.
- Give only the information that is asked for.
- Answer as clearly as possible.
- Leave time to proofread your response or essay.

How to Read Maps and Diagrams

Informational texts often use maps, diagrams, graphs, and charts. These tools help illustrate and explain the topic.

Maps

Maps show the location of places such as countries, states, and cities. They can also show where mountains, rivers, lakes, and streets are located. A compass rose on the map shows which way is north. A scale shows how miles or kilometers are represented on the map.

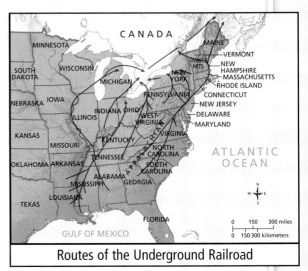

Routes of the Underground Railroad

Diagrams

Diagrams are drawings that explain things or show how things work. Some diagrams show pictures of how objects look on the outside or on the inside. Others show the different steps in a process.

This diagram shows the steps of the Scientific Method. It helps you understand the order and importance of each step.

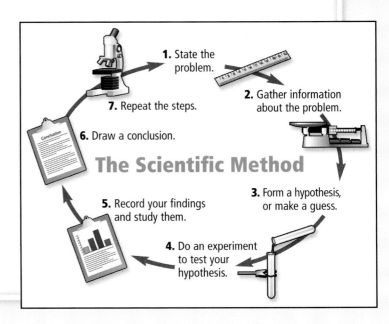

1. State the problem.
2. Gather information about the problem.
7. Repeat the steps.
6. Draw a conclusion.

The Scientific Method

3. Form a hypothesis, or make a guess.
5. Record your findings and study them.
4. Do an experiment to test your hypothesis.

How to Read Graphs

Graphs show how two or more kinds of information are related or alike. Three common kinds of graphs are **line graphs**, **bar graphs**, and **circle graphs**.

Line Graph

A **line graph** shows how information changes over a period of time. This line graph explains how the Native American population in Central Mexico changed over 100 years.

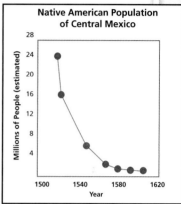

Bar Graphs

We use **bar graphs** to compare information. For example, this bar graph compares the populations of the 13 states in 1790.

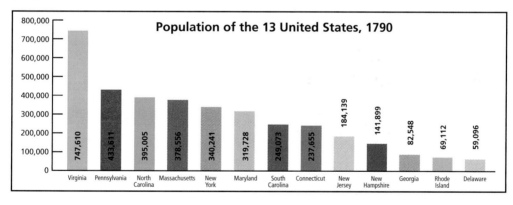

Circle Graphs

A **circle graph** is sometimes called a pie chart because it looks like a pie cut into slices. Circle graphs are used to show how different parts of a whole compare to each other.

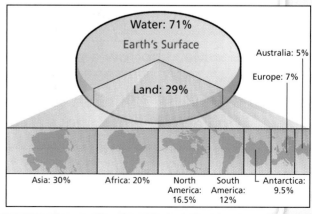

Parts of Speech

In English there are nine **parts of speech**: nouns, articles, pronouns, verbs, adjectives, adverbs, prepositions, conjunctions, and interjections.

Nouns

Nouns name people, places, or things.

A **common noun** is a general person, place, or thing.

> person   thing   place
> The **student** brings a **notebook** to **class**.

A **proper noun** is a specific person, place, or thing.

> person   place   thing
> **Joe** went to **Paris** and saw the **Eiffel Tower**.

Articles

Indefinite articles are *a* or *an*. They refer to a person, place, or thing.

Use *an* before a word that begins with a vowel sound.

> I have **an** idea.

Use *a* before a noun that begins with a consonant sound.

> May I borrow **a** pen?

The is called a **definite article**. Use *the* to talk about specific people, places, or things.

> Please bring me **the** box from your room.

Pronouns

Pronouns are words that take the place of nouns or proper nouns.

> proper noun   pronoun
> **Ana** is not home. **She** is babysitting.

	Subject Pronouns	**Object Pronouns**
Singular	I, you, he, she, it	me, you, him, her, it
Plural	we, you, they	us, you, them

A **subject pronoun** replaces the subject of a sentence. A **subject** is who or what a sentence is about.

> subject   subject pronoun (singular)
> **Dan** is a student. **He** goes to school every day.

Object pronouns replace a noun or proper noun that is the object of a verb. An **object** receives the action of a verb.

>   object   object pronoun (singular)
> Lauren gave **Ed** the notes. Lauren gave **him** the notes.

Possessive pronouns replace nouns or proper nouns. They show who owns something.

	Possessive Pronouns
Singular	mine, yours, hers, his
Plural	ours, yours, theirs

Verbs

Verbs express an action or a state of being.

An **action verb** tells what someone or something does or did.

Verbs That Tell Actions You Can See	Verbs That Tell Actions You Cannot See
dance swim	know sense

A **linking verb** shows no action. It links the subject with another word that describes the subject.

Examples of Linking Verbs		
look	smell	is
are	appear	seem

A helping verb comes before the main verb. They add to a verb's meaning.

	Helping Verbs
Forms of the verb *be*	am, was, is, were, are
Forms of the verb *do*	do, did, does
Forms of the verb *have*	have, had, has
Other helping verbs	can, must, could, have (to), should, may, will, would

Adjectives

Adjectives describe nouns. An adjective usually comes before the noun it describes.

> **tall** grass   **big** truck

An adjective can come *after* the noun it describes. This happens in these kinds of sentences.

> The bag is **heavy**. The books are **new**.

Adverbs

Adverbs describe the action of verbs. They tell *how* an action happens. Adverbs answer the question *Where?, When?, How?, How much?,* or *How often?*

Many adverbs end in *-ly*.

> easily   slowly

Some adverbs do not end in *-ly*.

> seldom   fast   very

In this sentence, the adverb *everywhere* modifies the verb *looked*. It answers the question *Where?*

>   verb   adverb
> Nicole looked **everywhere** for her book.

Prepositions

Prepositions show time, place, and direction.

Time	Place	Direction
after	above	across
before	below	down

In this sentence, the preposition *above* shows where the bird flew. It shows place.

> preposition
> A bird flew **above** my head.

In this sentence, the preposition *across* shows direction.

> preposition
> The children walked **across** the street.

A **prepositional phrase** starts with a preposition and ends with a noun or pronoun. In this sentence, the preposition is *near* and the noun is *school*.

> prepositional phrase
> The library is **near the new school**.

Conjunctions

A **conjunction** joins words, groups of words, and whole sentences. Common conjunctions include *and*, *but*, and *or*.

The conjunction *and* joins two proper nouns: *Allison* and *Teresa*.

> proper noun   proper noun
> Allison **and** Teresa are in school.

The conjunction *or* joins two prepositional phrases: *to the movies* and *to the mall*.

>   prepositional phrase   prepositional phrase
> They want to go to the movies **or** to the mall.

The conjunction *but* joins two independent clauses.

> independent clause   independent clause
> Alana baked the cookies, **but** Eric made the lemonade.

Interjections

Interjections are words or phrases that express emotion.

Interjections that express strong emotion are followed by an exclamation point.

> **Wow!** Did you see that catch?

A comma follows interjections that express mild emotion.

> **Gee**, I'm sorry that your team lost.

Sentences

Clauses

Clauses are groups of words with a subject and a verb.

- An **independent clause** can stand on its own as a complete sentence.
- A **dependent clause** cannot stand alone as a complete sentence.

Sentences

A simple sentence is an independent clause. It has a subject and a verb.

> subject   verb
> The dog barked.

A **compound sentence** is made up of two or more simple sentences, or independent clauses.

> ┌─── independent clause ───┐   ┌─── independent clause ───┐
> The band has a lead singer, **but** they need a drummer.

Sentence Types

Declarative sentences are statements. They end with a period.

> We are going to the beach on Saturday.

Interrogative sentences are questions. They end with a question mark.

> Will you come with us?

Imperative sentences are commands. They end with a period or an exclamation point.

> Put on your life jacket. Now jump in the water!

Exclamatory sentences express strong feeling. They end with an exclamation point.

> I swam all the way from the boat to the shore!

Punctuation

End Marks

End marks come at the end of sentences. There are three kinds of end marks: periods, question marks, and exclamation points.

Periods

- Use a period to end a statement (declarative sentence).
- Use a period to end a command or request (imperative sentence).
- Use a period after a person's initial or abbreviated title.
- Use a period after abbreviations.

Question Marks and Exclamation Points

- Use an exclamation point to express strong feelings.
- Use a question mark at the end of a question.

Commas

Commas separate parts of a sentence or phrase.

- Use a comma to separate two independent clauses linked by a conjunction.
- Use commas to separate the parts in a series. A series is a group of three or more words, phrases, or clauses.
- Use a comma to set off introductory words or phrases.
- Use commas to set off an interrupting word or phrase.
- Use a comma to set off a speaker's quoted words.
- Use commas to set off the name of the person being addressed in a letter or speech.

Semicolons and Colons

Semicolons can connect two independent clauses. Use them when the clauses are closely related in meaning or structure.

Colons introduce a list of items or important information. Also use a colon to separate hours and minutes when writing the time.

Quotation Marks

Quotation marks set off direct quotations, dialogue, and some titles.

- Commas and periods always go inside quotation marks.
- If a question mark or exclamation point is not part of the quotation, it goes outside the quotation marks.
- Use quotation marks to set off what people say in a dialogue.
- Use quotation marks around the titles of short works of writing.

Apostrophes

Apostrophes can be used with singular and plural nouns to show ownership or possession. To form the possessive, follow these rules:

- For singular nouns, add an apostrophe and an *s*.
- For singular nouns that end in *s*, add an apostrophe and an *s*.
- For plural nouns that do not end in *s*, add an apostrophe and an *s*.
- For plural nouns that end in *s*, add an apostrophe.
- Apostrophes are also used in contractions, to show where a letter or letters have been taken away.

Capitalization

There are five main reasons to use capital letters:

- to begin a sentence
- to write the pronoun *I*
- to write the names of proper nouns
- to write a person's title
- to write the title of a work (artwork, written work)

Modes of Writing

Narration is used to tell a story. Here are some types of narration.

- Autobiography is the story of a person's life, told by the writer.
- Biography is the story of a person's life told by another person.
- A short story is a short, fictional narrative.

Exposition gives information or explains something. Here are some types of exposition.

- Compare and Contrast writing analyzes the similarities and differences between two or more things.
- Cause and Effect writing explains why something happened and what happens as a result.
- Problem and Solution writing describes a problem and offers one or more solutions to it.
- How-To writing explains how to do or make something.
- Description paints a picture of a person, place, thing, or event.

Persuasion is writing that tries to convince people to think or act in a certain way.

Functional writing is writing for real-world uses. Here are some types of functional writing.

- You might fill out a form to sign up for lessons, take a field trip, or apply for a library card.
- You might create an invitation to a holiday party.

The Writing Process

The writing process is a series of steps that helps you write clearly.

Step 1: Pre-write

When you pre-write, you explore ideas and choose a topic. You identify your audience, and you choose your purpose for writing.

To choose a topic, try one or more of these strategies.

- **List** many ideas that you might want to write about.
- **Freewrite** about some ideas for five minutes.
- **Brainstorm** a list of ideas with a partner.

To identify your audience, think about who will read your writing. What do they already know? What do you need to explain?

To identify your purpose for writing, ask:

- Do I want to entertain my audience?
- Do I want to inform my audience?
- Do I want to persuade my audience?

Now, decide on the best form for your writing. Gather and organize the details that will support your topic.

Step 2: Draft

You start writing in this step. Put your ideas into sentences. Put your sentences into paragraphs. Begin to put your paragraphs in order. Don't worry too much about grammar and spelling. You will have a chance to correct any errors later.

Step 3: Revise

This is the time to look at your ideas and the organization of your writing. Read your first draft. Ask yourself:

- Are the ideas presented in the best order?
- Is there a clear beginning, middle, and end?
- Does each paragraph have a main idea and supporting details?

Ask a partner to read your writing and make comments about it. This is called a peer review. Decide what changes you want to make. Then rewrite your draft.

Step 4: Edit/Proofread

This is the time to look at word choice, sentence fluency, and writing conventions. Reread your paper. Proofread for mistakes in spelling, grammar, and punctuation. Correct any mistakes you find.

When you edit and proofread your draft, use these proofreading marks to mark the changes.

Editing/Proofreading Marks		
To:	**Use This Mark:**	**Example:**
add something	∧	We ate rice, bean, and corn.
delete something	℮	We ate rice, beans, and corns.
start a new paragraph	¶	¶ We ate rice, beans, and corn.
add a comma	∧,	We ate rice, beans and corn.
add a period	⊙	We ate rice, beans, and corn⊙
switch letters or words	∼	We ate rice, baens, and corn.
change to a capital letter	a̰	we ate rice, beans, and corn.
change to a lowercase letter	A̸	WE ate rice, beans, and corn.

Proofreading Checklist

- Check your spelling. Look up words you aren't sure of in the dictionary.
- Check your grammar and usage. Use the Grammar Handbook to help you correct sentences.
- Review capitalization and punctuation. Make sure each sentence begins with a capital letter and uses proper end punctuation.

Step 5: Publish

Once you have revised and proofread your paper, share it with others. Look at these publishing ideas.

- Post your paper on the bulletin board.
- Photocopy your paper. Hand it out to your classmates and family members.
- Attach it to an email and send it to friends.
- Sent it to a school newspaper or magazine for possible publication.

Once you have shared your work with others, you may want to put it in your portfolio. A portfolio is a folder or envelope in which you keep your writing. If you keep your work in a portfolio, you can look at what you have written over a period of time. This will let you see if your writing is improving. It will help you become a better writer.

Build Your Portfolio

You may want to keep your completed writing in your portfolio. It is a good idea to keep your drafts, too. Keep comments you receive from your teacher or writing partner, as well.

Reflect on Your Writing

Make notes on your writing in a journal. Write how you felt about what you wrote. Use these questions to help you get started.

- What new things did you learn about your topic?
- What helped you organize the details in your writing?
- What helped you revise your writing?
- What did you learn about yourself as you wrote?

Rubric for Writing

A rubric is a tool that helps you assess, or evaluate, your work. This rubric shows specific details for you to think about when you write. The scale ranges from 4 to 1, with 4 being the highest score and 1 being the lowest.

4	Writing is clearly focused on the task. Writing is well organized. Ideas follow a logical order. Main idea is fully developed and supported with details. Sentence structure is varied. Writing is free of fragments. There are no errors in writing conventions.
3	Writing is focused, with some unnecessary information. There is clear organization, with some ideas out of order. The main idea is supported, but development is uneven. Sentence structure is mostly varied, with some fragments. Writing conventions are generally followed.
2	Writing is related to the task but lacks focus. Organization is not clear. Ideas do not fit well together. There is little or no support for the main idea. No variation in sentence structure. Fragments occur often. Frequent errors in writing conventions.
1	The writing is generally unfocused. There is little organization or development. There is no clear main idea. Sentence structure is unvaried. There are many fragments. Many errors in writing conventions and spelling.

Writing and Research

Sometimes when you write, you need to do research to learn more information about your topic. You can do research in the library, on the Internet, and by viewing or listening to information media.

Library Reference

Encyclopedias contain basic facts, background information, and suggestions for additional research.

Biographical references provide brief life histories of famous people in many different fields.

Almanacs contain facts and statistics about many subjects, including government, world history, geography, entertainment, business, and sports.

Periodicals are past editions of magazines. Use a periodical index to find articles on your topic.

Vertical files contain pamphlets on a wide variety of topics.

Electronic databases provide quick access to information on many topics.

Citing Sources

When you do research, you read what other people wrote. The material you research is called the source or reference. When you tell who wrote the material, this is called citing the source. It is important to cite each source you use when you write.

In your paper, note each place in which you use a source. At the end of the paper, provide a list that gives details about all your sources. A bibliography and a works cited list are two types of source lists.

- A **bibliography** provides a listing of all the material you used during your research.

- A **works cited list** shows the sources you have quoted in your paper.

> **Plagiarism**
> Plagiarism is presenting someone else's words, ideas, or work as your own. If the idea or words are not yours, be sure to give credit by citing the source in your work. It is a serious offense to plagiarize.

Look at the chart of the Modern Language Association (MLA). Use this format for citing sources. This is the most common format for papers written by middle and high school students, as well as college students.

MLA Style for Listing Sources

Book	Pyles, Thomas. *The Origins and Development of the English Language*. 2nd ed. New York: Harcourt Brace Jovanovich, Inc., 1971.
Signed article in a magazine	Gustaitis, Joseph. "The Sticky History of Chewing Gum." *American History* Oct. 1998: 30–38.
Filmstrips, slide programs, videocassettes, DVDs	*The Diary of Anne Frank*. Dir. George Stevens. Perf. Millie Perkins, Shelly Winters, Joseph Schildkraut, Lou Jacobi, and Richard Beymer. Twentieth Century Fox, 1959.
Internet	*National Association of Chewing Gum Manufacturers*. 19 Dec. 1999. <http://www.nacgm.org/consumer/funfacts.html> [Indicate the date you found the information.]
Newspaper	Thurow, Roger. "South Africans Who Fought for Sanctions Now Scrap for Investors." *Wall Street Journal* 11 Feb. 2000.
Personal interview	Smith, Jane. Personal interview. 10 Feb. 2000.

Internet Research

The Internet is an international network of computers. The World Wide Web is a part of the Internet that lets you find and read information.

To do research on the Internet, you need to open a search engine. Type in a keyword on the search engine page. **Keywords** are words or phrases on the topic you want to learn about. For example, if you are looking for information about your favorite musical group, you might use the band's name as a keyword.

To choose a keyword, write a list of all the words you are considering. Then choose a few of the most important words.

Tips
- Spell the keywords correctly.
- Use the most important keyword first, followed by the less important ones.
- Open the pages at the top of the list first. These will usually be the most useful sources.

 How to Evaluate Information from the Internet

When you do research on the Internet, you need to be sure the information is correct. Use the checklist to decide if you can trust the information on a Web site.

✔ Look at the address bar. A URL that ends in "edu" is connected to a school or university. A URL that ends in "gov" means it is a site posted by a state or federal government. These sites should have correct information.

✔ Check that the people who write or are quoted on the site are experts, not just people telling their ideas or opinions.

✔ Check that the site is free of grammatical and spelling errors. This is often a hint that the site was carefully designed and researched.

✔ Check that the site is not trying to sell a product or persuade people.

✔ If you are not sure about using a site as a source, ask an adult.

Information Media

Media is all the organizations that provide news and information for the public. Media includes television, radio, and newspapers. This chart describes several forms of information media.

Types of Information Media	
Television News Program	• Covers current news events • Gives information objectively
Documentary	• Focuses on one topic of social interest • Sometimes expresses controversial opinions
Television Newsmagazine	• Covers a variety of topics • Entertains and informs
Radio Talk Show	• Covers some current events • Offers a place for people to express opinions
Newspaper Article	• Covers one current event • Gives details and background about the event
Commercial	• Presents products, people, or ideas • Persuades people to buy or take action

How to Evaluate Information from Various Media

Because the media presents large amounts of information, it is important to learn how to analyze this information. Some media sources try to make you think a certain way instead of giving you all the facts. Use these techniques to figure out whether you can trust information from the media.

✓ Sort facts from opinions. A fact is a statement that can be proven true. An opinion is how someone feels or thinks about something. Make sure any opinions are supported by facts.

✓ Be aware of the kind of media you are watching, reading, or listening to. Is it news or a documentary? Is it a commercial? What is its purpose?

✓ Watch out for bias. **Bias** is when the source gives information from only one point of view. Try to gather information from several points of view.

✓ Discuss what you learn from different media with your classmates or teachers. This will help you determine if you can trust the information.

✓ Read the entire article or watch the whole program before reaching a conclusion. Then, develop your own views on the issues, people, and information presented.

How To Use Technology in Writing

Writing on a Computer

You can write using a word processing program. This will help you when you follow the steps in the Writing Process.

- When you write your first draft, save it as a document.
- As you type or revise, you can move words and sentences using the cut, copy, and paste commands.
- When you proofread, you can use the grammar and spell check functions to help you check your work.

Keeping a Portfolio

Create folders to save your writing in. For example, a folder labeled "Writing Projects—September" can contain all of the writing you do during that month.

Save all the drafts of each paper you write.

Computer Tips

- Rename each of your revised drafts using the SAVE AS function. For example, if your first draft is "Cats," name the second draft "Cats2."
- If you share your computer, create a folder for only your work.
- Always back up your portfolio on a server or a CD.

Glossary

A

accommodate have enough space for (p. 247)

alter change (p. 233)

amenities things in a place that make living there enjoyable (p. 246)

appreciate be grateful for something (p. 141)

architecture shape and style of buildings (p. 218)

area place or location (p. 299)

ash gray powder that is left after something has been burned (p. 64)

astronaut someone who travels in space (p. 270)

attraction something interesting or fun to see or do (p. 194)

aware know about (p. 287)

B

bare empty; not covered by anything (p. 140)

bolt white line that appears in the sky (p. 92)

bond special relationship or connection (p. 39)

breath air that you let in and out through your nose and mouth (p. 38)

breeze light wind (p. 78)

C

campaign series of actions done to get a result, especially in business or politics (p. 180)

candidates people who hope to be chosen for a job or a political position (p. 180)

canyon deep valley with very steep sides (p. 298)

capital city in a country where the main government is (p. 26)

climate weather that a place usually has (p. 232)

comforts all the things that make your life easier (p. 246)

commit say that you will definitely do something (p. 181)

communicates speaks or writes to someone (p. 8)

companion person you are with, often a friend (p. 38)

conduct carry; allow electricity to pass through it (p. 93)

351

confirm show or say that something is true (p. 27)

construction process of building something (p. 169)

convince make someone believe something is true (p. 195)

council group of people who are chosen to make laws and decisions in a town or city (p. 126)

crater round open top of a volcano (p. 64)

creative good at making new and interesting things (p. 168)

D

dedicated working very hard at something because you think it is important (p. 26)

design drawing or plan (p. 247)

despite although something is true (p. 169)

dinosaur animal that lived a long time ago and no longer exists (p. 114)

domestic living on a farm or in a house (p. 233)

duty something you must do because it is right or part of your job (p. 126)

E

efficient working well, quickly, and without waste (p. 218)

electricity kind of energy (p. 92)

emerge appear or come out from somewhere (p. 127)

enormous very large (p. 195)

ensure make sure (p. 181)

eruption explosion (p. 64)

evaporate when a liquid turns into a gas (p. 92)

evidence proof (p. 65)

executive part of government that approves laws and organizes how they will work (p. 26)

explorer someone who travels into an unknown area to find out about it (p. 270)

extinct extinct plant or animal no longer exists (p. 114)

extreme very great (p. 218)

F

fair place where people, especially children, ride on special machines and play games to win prizes (p. 194)

fine very nice or of high quality (p. 140)

fossils parts of animals or plants that lived millions of years ago, or the shapes of these plants and animals that are now preserved in rocks (p. 114)

frisky full of energy, happiness, and fun (p. 38)

glowed shined with a steady light (p. 38)

government people who control what happens in a country (p. 180)

harsh very unpleasant; cruel (p. 232)

hiking taking a long walk in the country or in the mountains (p. 298)

hurricane storm with very strong fast winds (p. 78)

involve include, or be part of (p. 9)

justify give a good reason for (p. 271)

lava very hot liquid rock that comes out of the top of a mountain (p. 64)

law rule made by the government that all people must obey (p. 180)

ledge narrow flat surface of rock that is high above the ground (p. 298)

lightning bright flash of light in the sky that happens during a storm (p. 78)

link connection (p. 115)

locate find (p. 115)

major big or important (p. 79)

memorabilia things that you keep or collect because they relate to a famous person, event, or time (p. 26)

memories things that you remember about the past (p. 286)

mining digging in the ground for coal, iron, gold, etc. (p. 218)

mischief bad behavior, especially by children (p.126)

mission important job that someone has been given to do (p. 270)

muscles parts of your body under your skin which make you strong and help you to move (p. 114)

museum building where you can see old, interesting, or beautiful things (p. 26)

native growing or living in a particular place (p. 218)

natural not made by people or machines (p. 246)

nest move into a comfortable position (p. 246)

nonsense ideas or behaviors that are not true or seem stupid or annoying (p. 126)

objects things you can see, hold, or touch (p. 286)

occur happen (p. 271)

office important job or position in government (p. 180)

opportunity chance to do something (p. 194)

partner someone who works with you in an activity (p. 39)

persuade make someone decide to do something by giving him or her good reasons (p. 194)

plaque piece of flat metal or stone with writing on it (p. 270)

politics activities or opinions concerned with how power is used in the government of a country (p. 180)

prairie large open area of land that is covered in wheat or long grass (p. 232)

pride feeling of pleasure or satisfaction that you have because of something good that you have done (p. 286)

protect prevent someone or something from being harmed or damaged (p. 8)

pursue chase or follow (p. 299)

R

record information that is written down so you can look at it later (p. 232)

region large land area (p. 79)

reject not accept (p. 287)

require need something (p. 9)

research careful study, usually to find out new facts about something (p. 194)

reside live somewhere (p. 27)

reuse use something again (p. 168)

roam walk or travel in a place (p. 286)

rural relating to the country, not the city (p. 168)

S

salvage save something from a situation in which other things have already been damaged, destroyed, or lost (p. 168)

sandstone type of soft yellow or red rock (p. 114)

satisfied pleased because something has happened in the way that you want (p. 126)

secure safe (p. 8)

security protection from harm or loss; safety (p. 93)

shelter protect from bad weather or danger (p. 78)

shimmer shine with a soft light that seems to shake slightly (p. 38)

signatures people's names, written in their own handwriting (p. 270)

similar almost the same, but not exactly (p. 65)

sod piece of dirt with grass growing on top (p. 232)

species group of plants or animals of the same type (p. 114)

stitches small lines of thread sewn onto cloth (p. 140)

stroke particular moment or movement (p. 140)

structures buildings (p. 246)

suggested told someone that something is a good idea (p. 194)

surrounded have a lot of a particular type of people or things near you (p. 270)

survive stay alive (p. 219)

temperature how hot or cold something is (p. 92)

thrilling exciting and interesting (p. 298)

thrive be very strong and healthy (p. 298)

thunder loud sound that you hear in the sky during a storm (p. 78)

tidbit small piece of food or information (p. 126)

trails paths across open country, or through mountains or woods (p. 298)

transmit send or pass (p. 127)

treasures valuable things (p. 286)

underground under Earth's surface (p. 218)

unique one of a kind (p. 219)

unusual not usual or ordinary; strange (p. 26)

urban relating to a town or city (p. 168)

vacant empty (p. 168)

valuable worth a lot of money (p. 286)

volcano mountain with a hole at the top from which come burning rock and fire (p. 64)

voluntary done willingly without expecting payment or reward (p. 141)

warm slightly hot, but not too hot (p. 38)

whisk quickly take something or someone somewhere (p. 140)

wink close and open one eye quickly (p. 140)

Y

young not old; not having lived very long (p. 8)

Index

Credits

Bettmann/CORBIS; 187 bottom, Bettmann/CORBIS; 188, Omni-Photo Communications; 191, AP Wide World Photos; 192, PhotoEdit; 194 top, image100/Corbis/PunchStock; 194 bottom, Timothy G. Laman/National Geographic Society/Getty Images; 195 top, Ambient Images; 195 bottom, Jack Hollingsworth/Corbis/PunchStock; 196 Digital Vision; 197, Art Resource NY; 198 left, The Granger Collection, NY; 198 right, The Granger Collection, NY; 199 ©B. W. Kilburn/Corbis; 201, Carey B. Van Loon; 202 PhotoEdit; 203 The Granger Collection, NY; 204 Stone Allstock/Getty Images; 206-207 Jack Anthony; 207 Robert W. Ginn/PhotoEdit; 208 top, The Granger Collection, NY; 208 bottom, ©Steve Nudson/Alamy; 209 top, Jupiter Images; 209 bottom, AP/Wide World Photos.

UNIT 5: 212-213 Courtney Kolar/Alamy; 212 left, ©Alessandro Gandolfi/Index Stock Imagery; 212 middle, Library of Congress; 212 right, PhotoEdit; 213 ©Beat Blanzmann/Corbis; 215 top right, PhotoEdit; 215 top middle, PhotoEdit; 215 bottom middle, Dorling Kindersley; 215 bottom Dorling Kindersley; 216 left, Carl & Ann Purcell/Corbis; 216 left inset, Ellen Senisi; 216 right, Albrecht G. Schaefer/Corbis; 216 right inset, Digital Stock/CORBIS; 217 bottom, Lamar Koethe; 217 bottom inset, Photo Researchers; 217 top, Gillian Darley; Edifice/Corbis; 217 top inset, Catherine Karnow/Corbis; 218 top, Frans Lanting/Corbis; 218 bottom left, Dorling Kindersley; 218 bottom right, National Geographic; 219 top left, Dorling Kindersley; 219 top right, Dorling Kindersley; 219 middle, The Image Works; 219 bottom, Studio DL/Corbis/PunchStock; 220-221 Getty Images; 221 top, ©Alessandro Gandolfi/Index Stock Imagery; 221 bottom, ©R. Ian Lloyd/Masterfile Corporation; 222 top, ©Paul A. Souders/Corbis; 222 bottom, The Granger Collection, NY; 223 top, ©Paul A. Souders/Corbis; 223 bottom, ©Paul A. Souders/Corbis; 224 top left, Photo Researchers; 224 top right, Creative Eye/MIRA; 224 middle, Photo Researchers; 224 bottom, Photo Researchers; 225 top, Photo Researchers; 225 middle, Creative Eye/MIRA; 225 bottom, Photo Researchers; 226 John Carnemolla/Australian Picture Library/Corbis; 228 ©R. Ian Lloyd/Masterfile Corporation; 230 Ester Beaton/Corbis; 232 top, Dorling Kindersley; 232 middle, Dorling Kindersley; 232 bottom, Taxi/Getty Images; 233 top, Robert Fried Photography; 233 bottom, PhotoEdit; 234-235 ©David Muench/Corbis; 234 Library of Congress; 235 ©James L. Amos/Corbis; 236-237 Getty Images; 236 Library of Congress; 237 ©Royalty-Free/Corbis; 238 ©David Muench/Corbis; 238 inset; Solomon D. Butcher/Library of Congress; 239 ©Tom Bean/Corbis; 239 inset, ©Philip Gould/Corbis; 240 Bettmann/CORBIS; 241 Nebraska State Historical Society; 242 Bettmann/CORBIS; 244 Nebraska State Historical Society; 245 Nebraska State Historical Society; 246 top, Chris Carroll/Corbis; 246 middle, Atlantide Phototravel/Corbis; 246 bottom, Photodisc/Getty Images; 247 top, Tim Street-Porter/Beateworks/Corbis; 247 bottom, Getty Images; 247 top, Getty Images; 248 Photodisc/Getty Images; 249 PhotoEdit; 250 left, The Stock Connection; 250 right, Paul Rocheleau; 251 Omni-Photo Communications; 252 Thomas Fricke/Corbis; 254 Peter Estersohn/Beateworks/Corbis; 255 Anders Ryman/Corbis; 256 David P. Hall/Corbis; 258 top, ©Galen Rowell/Corbis; 258 bottom, ©Tom Van Sant/Corbis; 259 top, Vincent Lowe/Alamy Images; 259 bottom, ©Beat Blanzmann/Corbis; 260 top, ©Staffan Widstrand/Corbis; 260 bottom, ©Rob Howard/Corbis; 261 top, ©Peter Harholdt/Corbis; 261 bottom, ©Robert van der Hilst/Corbis.

UNIT 6: 264-265 Corbis/PunchStock; 265 Getty Images; 267 top right, Pearson Education Corporate Digital Archive; 267 top middle, Dorling Kindersley; 267 bottom middle, Dorling Kindersley; 267 bottom right, Robert Harding World Imagery; 268 left, Pearson Education/PH College; 268 left